Anchored

Anchored

A Bible Study for
Miscarriage, Stillbirth, & Infant Loss

Erin Cushman

WESTBOW
PRESS®
A DIVISION OF THOMAS NELSON
& ZONDERVAN

WestBow Press books may be ordered through booksellers or by contacting:

WestBow Press
A Division of Thomas Nelson & Zondervan
1663 Liberty Drive
Bloomington, IN 47403
www.westbowpress.com
1 (866) 928-1240

Because of the dynamic nature of the Internet, any web addresses or links contained in this book may have changed since publication and may no longer be valid. The views expressed in this work are solely those of the author and do not necessarily reflect the views of the publisher, and the publisher hereby disclaims any responsibility for them.

Any people depicted in stock imagery provided by Thinkstock are models, and such images are being used for illustrative purposes only. Certain stock imagery © Thinkstock.

Unless otherwise indicated, Scripture is from the ESV® Bible (The Holy Bible, English Standard Version®), copyright © 2001 by Crossway Bibles, a publishing ministry of Good News Publishers. Used by permission. All rights reserved.

Scripture quotations marked NIV are from The Holy Bible: New International Version®, NIV®. Copyright © 1973, 1978, 1984 by Biblica, Inc.™ Used by permission. All rights reserved worldwide.

All emphases in Scripture quotations have been added by the author. Artwork by Constance Ray at CRay Designs.

ISBN: 978-1-5127-0766-3 (sc)
ISBN: 978-1-5127-0767-0 (hc)
ISBN: 978-1-5127-0768-7 (e)

Library of Congress Control Number: 2015914130

Print information available on the last page.

WestBow Press rev. date: 12/28/2015

For the courageous Hope Moms and Dads who have
faithfully endured heartache, awaiting the day when
they will see their beloved child once more.

And for Gwendolyn, my precious reminder of our blessed Hope.

Every day is one day closer.

CONTENTS

ACKNOWLEDGMENTS

To the Circle of Hope donors who made this publication possible: we are deeply grateful for your generosity and commitment to the spread of biblical truth. Silver and gold level donations were given in honor of Regina Walker and her babies, Baby Fuchs, Carter Wells, Evan Rush Southard, Ella Jane Jones, the Don Nelson family, Baby Scott, Baby Ray, and Gwendolyn Hope Cushman.

To Elyse, Michelle, Sarah, Corrie, Ashlee, Kelly, Lauren, Lianna, and Chelsea: thank you for sharing the stories of your precious children and the way the Lord has used their lives to shape yours. I am so eager to meet your little ones one day soon.

To Constance: your compassion, creativity, and obedience gave us roots. Never doubt the gift of mercy that you've been given or the way it has changed so many.

To the Hope Mommies leadership team: your dedication, empathy, and service have been invaluable to the spread of the gospel across the world (quite literally), as we share the hope that we cling to. I love each of you and am so honored to stand in the gap with you.

To Blair: we have grieved well. I'm grateful that as the Lord has used our marriage to grow us in holiness, He's given us so much happiness along the way. Our joy is sweeter for having known so much pain. I love you and can't imagine this life without you.

ABOUT HOPE MOMMIES

Blair and Erin Cushman founded Hope Mommies in 2011, a few months after the death of their newborn daughter, Gwendolyn Hope Cushman. Hope Mommies is a 501(c)3 nonprofit Christian organization. The mission is this:

> to share the hope of Christ with bereaved mothers
> and families experiencing infant loss.

Through their box ministry, social media, hope groups, and retreats, Hope Mommies has served thousands of Hope Moms and families by providing a safe, biblical community for those grieving. Hope Mommies is equipping the outside community to serve the brokenhearted and is raising awareness about infant loss.

To learn more about Hope Mommies, visit www.hopemommies.org.

INTRODUCTION

Dear Friend,

I don't know the particular circumstances that have caused you to pick up this book, but I can only imagine that in some way you have been touched by pregnancy or infant loss. It is a profound grief, and I mourn with you.

My firstborn, Gwendolyn, went to be with Jesus just thirty-six hours after she was born. Letting go of her was the most excruciating event of my life, and it left me with a shattered heart. I was confused and distraught; I was without a "plan." Everything I had hoped for had been stripped away.

A verse from 2 Timothy reverberated within my heart as I sat in the hospital bed, shell-shocked by my circumstances. "For I know whom I have believed, and I am convinced that he is able to guard until that Day what has been entrusted to me" (2 Timothy 1:12 ESV). I knew that God was still the same God from forty-eight hours ago when she was alive and well within my womb. But I was lost in grief, feeling alone and unsure how to relate to a God that allowed my infant daughter to die.

In the days, weeks, and months following her heaven-going, the Lord surrounded me with an encouraging group of women who had also experienced loss. Together we pressed in to God's Word and to each other. Hope Mommies was formed so that every grieving mom would have a safe group that could empathize with her and point her toward hope. This book is a culmination of the questions and comforts of these Hope Moms as we brought our raw grief and our requests before God, waiting on Him to answer.

This book works from the inside out. It begins with evaluating our understanding of God and His Word, His heaven, and the hope He offers us. Then it addresses the hard and tangible questions, such as these: How can I trust God again? How do I handle envy? How can I relate to my spouse? How can I interact with the non-grieving world around me? Each chapter offers you a chance to engage with God's Word and study it for yourself, and each chapter gives you space to journal your response. Precious stories from fellow Hope Moms are included, and I hope that you will find comfort knowing that you are not alone in your grief; you are journeying alongside many brave women as you inch your way toward eternity.

Whether you have never picked up a Bible or are well versed in the Scriptures, working through these questions can give encouragement, hope, and wisdom. God's Word is always fruitful and accomplishes His goal for those who read it (Isaiah 55:10–11). This book has been written to be used individually or with a small group, and a "Leader's Guide" is in the back to help assist with group discussions.

I'm praying that as you open this book and read the Bible alongside it, you will find truth and hope. Romans 5:5 says that a hope founded upon the love of God and salvation from God will not disappoint us. Knowing Him will change your life and will restore your hope and joy. I'm praying that this study will enable you to draw closer to His heart so that you will know Him and find comfort for your weary soul as you lean upon Him.

Because He lives, I hope.

Erin Cushman
Hope Mommies founder

REFLECTIONS

Use the space below to write out your own story.

At the beginning of our study together, I encourage you to ponder this question: How do I want this loss to shape the woman I become? In ten years, what five words do I want to describe me? Write your answers below.

CHAPTER 1

MARKED BY LOSS

 Your eyes saw my unformed substance;
in your book were written, every one of them,
the days that were formed for me,
when as yet there were none of them.
—Psalm 139:16

After my daughter fell asleep,[1] I felt as though I had "My daughter died" written in permanent marker across my forehead, as if I were a walking billboard for grief. I felt that even complete strangers should know that something was wrong with me! I was *marked*.

You are marked by loss. It's true that you will never be the same person you were before, but that doesn't mean you will always be as you are now. The life and death of your child will continue to have a profound impact on your heart, and that's a good thing. Your child's life was not an accident. He or she was planned and purposed by God, just as it was His plan to make you his or her parent. Psalm 139 is a beautiful illustration of how the Creator God has intimate knowledge of each and every life—yours and your hope baby's.

ENGAGING TRUTH

O LORD, you have searched me and known me!
You know when I sit down and when I rise up;
you discern my thoughts from afar.
You search out my path and my lying down
and are acquainted with all my ways.
Even before a word is on my tongue,
behold, O LORD, you know it altogether.
You hem me in, behind and before,
and lay your hand upon me.
Such knowledge is too wonderful for me;
it is high; I cannot attain it.
—Psalm 139:1–6

What does this teach us about God's knowledge?

Where shall I go from your Spirit?
Or where shall I flee from your presence?
If I ascend to heaven, you are there!
If I make my bed in Sheol, you are there!
If I take the wings of the morning
and dwell in the uttermost parts of the sea,
even there your hand shall lead me,
and your right hand shall hold me.
If I say, "Surely the darkness shall cover me,
and the light about me be night,"
even the darkness is not dark to you;
the night is bright as the day,
for darkness is as light with you.
—Psalm 139:7–12

What does this teach about God's presence?

For you formed my inward parts;
you knitted me together in my mother's womb.
I praise you, for I am fearfully and wonderfully made.
Wonderful are your works;
my soul knows it very well.
My frame was not hidden from you,
when I was being made in secret,
intricately woven in the depths of the earth.
Your eyes saw my unformed substance;
in your book were written, every one of them,
the days that were formed for me,
when as yet there was none of them.
How precious to me are your thoughts, O God!
How vast is the sum of them!
If I would count them, they are more than the sand.
I awake, and I am still with you.
—Psalm 139:13–18

What do verses 13–16 illuminate about God's purpose and His creation of each life?

What does this teach about the length of each life?

What do we learn about God's character from this passage?

This is a rich psalm that describes God's complete omniscience (His complete knowledge of everything, everywhere), His omnipresence (He is at all times present everywhere), and His authority and power to create and sustain life. Contemporary culture would have us believe that life doesn't begin until a baby takes his or her first breath—how wonderfully does this psalm undermine that idea! Your baby was perfectly planned by

God. He saw your little one and formed him or her just the way He wanted him or her to be formed. He gave your baby a soul and inherent value at the moment of conception.

God was not unaware of your distress the moment you learned that something was wrong with your precious one. He was fully aware and fully present in that moment. He did not turn a blind eye but was tenderly and compassionately caring for you and your baby.

Thank You, Father, for being an intimate, loving God who cares for His children. Your character is not limited. You see all, You know all, and what You have purposed will stand. Thank You that, though You've allowed us to be marked by loss, You have not abandoned us. Thank You for creating each hope baby and planning his or her life; we can find rest and comfort with You. Amen.

REFLECTIONS

Was there a particular verse that struck your heart as you read?

How was this psalm encouraging?

Write out your own prayer in response.

GOING DEEPER:

Write Psalm 139 on a card, and then put it on your bathroom mirror or in a place you will see and read it often.

EMMA'S STORY

The Lord has marked my life in many ways, but I have been deeply impacted by the loss of my daughter, Emma. Just as we were about to start fertility medication, we learned that we were expecting our first child. We were ecstatic, and the first trimester went so well! We were unaware of the gender, joking around as we went into our first-trimester screening.

We learned that day that something was very wrong and chose to have a chorionic villus sampling test performed. A few days later, the results revealed that our precious girl had Turner syndrome, a chromosomal condition that is not hereditary; her DNA was just missing a puzzle piece. We continued to diligently pray that the Lord's will would be done while begging to keep our daughter on earth. We continued to see various doctors as her health problems increased and clung to these truths from the Bible:

We know that God is still knitting our little girl together, and He knows exactly what He is doing (Psalm 139:13).

He doesn't make mistakes. He is perfect, and His will is perfect (Deuteronomy 32:4; Psalm 18:30; Matthew 5:48).

He has a great plan to prosper us and not to harm us, a plan to give us hope and a future (Jeremiah 29:11).

He gives us strength to do all things (Philippians 4:13).

We trust Him; He's got this (Psalms 9:10, 31:14, 56:3, 84:12; Isaiah 12:2).

At twenty-two weeks, our precious Emma Kate opened her eyes to meet Jesus. I delivered her a few days later. We wanted her name to be significant; Emma means "one who is complete," and Kate means "pure." We know that she is whole. She is perfect and complete. She has no pain. She is in the amazing presence of our precious Savior. We are so thankful that He blessed us with Emma. "The LORD gave, and the LORD has taken away; blessed be the name of the LORD" (Job 1:21).

Although our dreams for our precious daughter were shattered, our eyes were opened to so much. The Lord used our short time with Emma and many of our hardest days of grief to work in our lives and to soften our hearts to others in this broken world.

We have hope that one day we will be reunited with our precious, tiny one in glory. We are learning to accept that our hopes and dreams for our little one were not His plans for her. While our hearts ache, we remember and cling to these truths based on His Word:

"The LORD is near to the brokenhearted and saves the crushed in spirit" (Psalm 34:18).

Our great and mighty God *will* see us through this (Deuteronomy 31:8).

He is faithful, even in death and loss. "And we know that for those who love God all things work together for good, for those who are called according to his purpose" (Romans 8:28).

None of this has been a surprise to Him; it is just a tiny piece of His perfect plan for our lives (Jeremiah 29:11).

He will use Emma's life. He will make it beautiful, and He will use it to bring glory to Himself in amazing ways. Regardless of what we could possibly begin to understand, He is going to bring beauty from our pain (Ecclesiastes 3:11).

And most of all, "The *joy* of the LORD is your strength!" (Nehemiah 8:10). We pray that our present suffering will bring us closer to the heart of God and that our journey and lives would bring Him glory (John 9:3).

I am forever marked. Marked by loss, grief, and shattered dreams. But I am also marked by a sweet Savior's amazing grace and hope for eternity with Him. My dark, sin-filled heart was transformed to be as white as snow when I accepted Christ as my Savior. My life was marked by Him, but I have never clung so tightly to Him as I did during our roller-coaster ride of not knowing how long we would have Emma with us. Not only has my heart been changed by my experience with Emma, but also it has marked every aspect of my life—for the better.

Marked relationships: Grieving is tough and reveals truth in relationships. It was painful, yet comforting, to have superficial relationships stripped away and honest, genuine relationships deepened. I realized that my true friends would do, listen, and say absolutely anything. I love that they are the ones who will ask about my memories with Emma and brighten my heart by saying her name and honoring her in special ways. I realize now how much I lean on my family for support and how they generously love and care for me. My husband and I grieved very differently—who doesn't?—which was difficult. But our experience brought us closer to each other and allowed us to love each other in a new way.

Marked compassion: I now realize just how little I understand about what other people are going through. I probably have a little more patience and empathy in my interactions with others. We decided not to broadcast our experience until after Emma had died, just to attempt to keep *some* normalcy and avoid having a daily pity party, so people truly had no idea of the journey we were on. I remember sometimes wishing for a disappearing cape that would let me vanish from the relentless questions, parenting advice, daily chores, housekeeping, and all the other stuff. My heart has been softened to the guy who is daydreaming and sits through the entire green light, the lady who bursts into tears when she realizes she forgot to grab deodorant for her husband as she is checking out, and so forth. We truly never know what someone else is dealing with or trying to survive.

Marked priorities: A line from the hymn "Turn Your Eyes upon Jesus" summarizes this for me. "The things of earth grow strangely dim, in the light of His glory and grace." This type-A personality has chilled a bit. I realized during our journey what things really do matter to me. My priorities have shifted, and I think my demeanor has changed a little with it. I can still tend to be a perfectionist and get a little too focused on my to-do list, but overall I realize and take time for the important things. I focus more on the people in my life (the souls that I come in contact with each day, whether I know them or not). I care deeply about their salvation and relationship with the Lord. I want to care more for my friends and love of my family. I want to minister to other Hope Moms and people who are hurting. I want to be used by Him, and I want my priorities (and the things I spend my time on) to reflect that.

A marked faith: I have a stronger relationship with my King. Experiencing a deep sorrow, hardship, trial, or loss (whatever you want to call it) has allowed me to connect with the Lord on another level. I really hadn't experienced anything as difficult or devastating; I hadn't *had* to rely completely and utterly on Him. I also had to work through believing what I claimed to believe. It wasn't easy (He never said it would be), but He has continued to be faithful and good.

I pray that you will find the ways in which the Lord has marked your life through your salvation and through your loss. Sweet Hope Mom, I pray that you will allow Him to use your marked life to bring Him glory.

by Elyse Griffin, Hope Mom to Emma

CHAPTER 2

WHAT ABOUT GOD?

 My soul melts away for sorrow; strengthen
me according to your word!
—Psalm 119:28

I know you have experienced this truth: death shakes you to your core, unveiling your foundation and theology. When Gwenny went to the Lord, I felt completely wrecked, a huddled mess cowering before a reality that was just too horrible. I longed for some truth to anchor me and help me from completely losing it.

I don't think it's possible for your child to be hurt, dying, or already in heaven without your own heart crying out to God. You may not have even known God, talked to Him, or trusted Him before that moment, but I don't think it's possible for any human being to be in such a powerless situation without reaching out to Him for help.

A. W. Tozer said, "What comes into our minds when we think about God is the most important thing about us."[2] This means our whole lives are built upon a foundation of what we believe about God: *Is there a God? What is He like? Is He good? Does He involve Himself with us? What does He want from me?* What you believe about God will determine how you live, and especially how you grieve. Consider the following examples:

Jane believes that God is good—there isn't evil in Him—but she doesn't believe that He is in control of all things—that He is sovereign. Jane's god is like a nice big Santa Claus. He's jolly and well-intentioned but has no power. He cannot help her when difficulty or heartaches arise, because he has no ability to do so. Jane will grieve on her own, trying to make the best of her situation and to control everything at hand. Her marriage, living children, and friendships will suffer because Jane will try to manipulate the situations to achieve the results she desires.

Edith believes that God either doesn't exist or—if He does—He is unkind/unloving. Her god cannot help her, because she thinks that everything bad that happens is his fault. If her perception of God never changes, Edith will live within a victim mentality. Everything that happens to her is God's (or her husband's, or friend's, or family's) fault. Edith will not trust God or talk to God, because He doesn't have relevancy in her life.

Claire believes that God is good, even if her circumstances don't feel like goodness. She also believes that God is in control; that He can and does care about the daily moments and the big events of her life. Claire believes that God's Word trumps her experiences. She is building on a foundation that can last. Her marriage, friendships, and family can survive because she is leaning on someone who is both loving and sovereign. She does not have to have all the answers or control the relationships around her. Her good is wrapped up in His goodness.

In this chapter, we will be discussing three aspects about God that we must believe in order to have a solid, unshakable foundation that can hold up underneath the crushing weight of your baby's death: God's goodness, God's sovereignty (or power), and the sufficiency of God's Word, the Bible.

ENGAGING TRUTH

God's Goodness

> Every good gift and every perfect gift is from above, coming down
> from the Father of lights with whom there is no variation or shadow
> due to change.
> —James 1:17

Who is the author of good things? _____

What does it mean that God is the "Father of lights"?

Why is it a comfort to know that there is "no variation or shadow due to change" in God's character? What does that imply?

You are good and do good;
teach me your statutes.
—Psalm 119:68

The LORD is good,
a stronghold in the day of trouble.
—Nahum 1:7

I am the good shepherd. The good shepherd lays down his life for the sheep.
—John 10:11

What aspect of God's nature do these verses emphasize?

Wayne Grudem in his *Systematic Theology* defines God's goodness as follows: "The goodness of God means that God is the final standard of good, and that all that God is and does is worthy of approval."[3] Why is it important to have a firm grasp on God's goodness?

God's Sovereignty

Ah, Lord GOD! It is you who has made the heavens and the earth by your great power and by your outstretched arm! Nothing is too hard for you.
—Jeremiah 32:17

What does this reveal about God's abilities?

What is too difficult for God to handle?

God's Word Is Sufficient

> All Scripture is breathed out by God and profitable for teaching, for reproof, for correction, and for training in righteousness, that the man of God may be competent, equipped for every good work. —2 Timothy 3:16–17

Who is the ultimate author of Scripture (the Bible)? _____

Fill in the blanks: "profitable for _____, for _____, for _____, and for training in _____."

Is there anything in life to which the Bible cannot be applied?

What is the result for the man or woman who is taught, reproved, corrected, and trained by God's Word?

For the word of God is living and active, sharper than any two-edged sword, piercing to the division of soul and of spirit, of joints and of marrow, and discerning the thoughts and intentions of the heart. And no creature is hidden from his sight, but all are naked and exposed to the eyes of him to whom we must give account.
—Hebrews 4:12–13

What adjectives does the author use to describe the Bible?

Is there a boundary for God's Word? Anything that it cannot affect?

Because God is limitless, trying to summarize His character in just one chapter is impossible! But knowing these three things about Him is foundational to knowing Him. God is a good God who defines goodness and acts in goodness. Everything He does is good. God is a powerful and sovereign God and will work everything according to the counsel of His perfect will (Ephesians 1:11). And He communicated His character, His love, and His plan for salvation to us through His Word, the Bible. Because the Bible is authoritative and without error, it can apply and speak to every situation we find ourselves in. How comforting it is to know that God is good and in control and has given us a way to know Him.

Thank you, Abba, that Your goodness is infinite, Your power is supreme, and Your Word is sufficient for our every need. Would You please strengthen us according to Your Word, as we rest upon Your character? Amen.

REFLECTIONS

Are you more similar to Jane, Edith, or Claire from the previous examples of faith? How so? If not, why not?

Why is it vital to believe that God is both good and sovereign and that His Word is sufficient? Are you convinced these things are true? Why or why not?

If God were not in control of everything in the universe, then who or what is in control?

If God's Word did not have the answers to your problems and questions, then where else do you turn?

Which aspect of God's character is hard for you to swallow at times? Why is that? How can you align your thoughts and emotions to reflect what God's Word says on the subject?

GOING DEEPER:

Use whatever creative medium you prefer (paint, pencil, charcoal, clay, crayons, etc.), and draw a picture of your perception of your relationship to God right now.

JAXON'S STORY

I will always remember the way Jaxon constantly pushed up on my ribs. I could easily picture him pleading, "Mom, get off of me, pleeeeease! You're squishing me!" While coming up on six months, I had asked my midwife if she could guess how long he was because it was as if he never had enough room. I will never forget her know-it-all answer. "No, no, honey, you're just short!" *Yeah, we'll see* is what I thought as I knowingly smirked back at her in my head.

We chose to welcome Jaxon into this world at a birthing center in downtown Dallas. We felt safe there because we were fewer than three minutes from the big Baylor hospital. But what made me feel even safer was I knew I wouldn't be pressured into using Pitocin or an epidural or having an unnecessary C-section. I wanted a drug-free labor so that my baby would latch on immediately and we could successfully breast-feed for as long as we wanted.

We prepared as much as we could for the pain with an eight-week birthing class and had all of the pain-management techniques practiced and memorized. We were well prepared, so of course we thought nothing was going to happen that we hadn't already anticipated. Our son was growing and active and healthy. Everything was going great and we were in control.

The day I reached thirty-eight weeks, I went in for what I thought would be a quick checkup. My blood pressure was noticeably higher than the week before, so my midwife wanted to do a couple of extra checks. She started pressing on my belly, swooshing Jaxon around while trying to get a feel for his position and size. After surprisingly feeling that he was smaller than he should be, she scheduled a sonogram for me the same afternoon.

What they found was my amniotic fluid was low and Jaxon was measuring at only five and a half pounds. I thought, *No way that's possible!* After being lectured that I must have overworked myself in the last couple of weeks, I was ordered to go home on bed rest and drink lots of water. They would check me again in three days. If my fluid level didn't improve, I would be induced. I drank water nonstop because in my head I pictured I was building up my amniotic fluid and I was going to make it safe for Jaxon. We were still in control.

So there I was three days later, on the morning of November 12, back at the birthing center. I was sure that my fluid level had gone up and was anxious to hear that everything was back on track. All too quickly, my heart froze in fear as I heard the news that my fluid level dropped even further and they indeed were going to induce me. That awful "cry lump" had formed in my throat, and I thought my heart was going to beat right out of my chest, but I trusted that they were making the right call so I went along with the new plan. I could trust them. It would be fine. *Nobody loses a baby at this point. We are still in control.*

My midwife began the induction that day at noon, and I was told to go home and rest. I was to expect some cramping, but more than likely, I would not go into labor just yet. We planned to go back and see her in the morning after getting some sleep.

My labor actually began about four hours later, and by 12:45 a.m. we were at the birthing center in active labor. My midwife turned on the Doppler several minutes after we arrived and we started listening for Jaxon. His heartbeat had never been hard to find before, but she was struggling to find it. This wasn't happening. I wasn't even entertaining the thought of something so horrible.

The next thing I knew, I was in my midwife's car and rushing for the hospital, my husband following close behind. I still wasn't entertaining the thought. Jaxon was fine. I started to pray. Before we left, I told my husband to text everyone and ask them to **pray.** If we did this, everything would be fine. *God, please, this can't be happening. Just make everything okay.* And then her words pierced right through my bubble.

"Michelle, do you realize what is happening?" she asked, as if I was not acting the way I should be.

The sonogram room at Baylor was dim and cold. I climbed up on the table, lay down on my back, which was absolutely *the worst* position my laboring body wanted to be in, and grabbed for my husband's hand. I will never forget the fear in everyone's searching eyes. I have never heard a man wail the way my husband did when the doctor said, "I'm sorry. There is no heartbeat."

My husband knew his son. He loved to kiss the bottom of my belly where Jaxon's head was because Jaxon would always jump in response. What an amazing experience it is to watch your husband and son interact with each other before they can even see one another. The last time he did this was around 9:45 p.m. that night. We were almost there. *Babies just don't die like this; they don't.* I ate healthy, I exercised, I took all of my vitamins, and I avoided deli meats and soft cheeses! I did everything they told me to do, so why couldn't we prevent this? I did my part, now what about His part? *Where was God when Jaxon's heart stopped beating?*

I delivered my firstborn on November 13, 2013, just a week and a half shy of his due date. Jaxon was a healthy baby boy weighing six pounds and twelve ounces and measuring twenty-two inches long. I got confirmation of something that I already knew—Jaxon was not underweight and he was long! He looked just like his daddy, but I proudly claimed his little chin and feet. Oh, how I missed those baby toes. He was blessed with not just brown, not just blond, but also with red hair! Jaxon was perfect.

That day held our highest highs and our lowest lows. We finally saw and held our firstborn; it was a beautiful moment. But in the same day, we had to give him back. My faith in God and His promises were shaken to the core. How can a God that is good let my baby die? He knew Jaxon was in trouble and He had the power to fix it, but He didn't. The house I had built with God fell that day.

I began to let anger, blame, and guilt hang over my head. The guilt I believe was the hardest to handle. The comments people can innocently (and sometimes not so innocently) make after knowing you labored at home can sting something awful, and they stirred up even more guilt than I already had. I not only blamed my body for crushing his umbilical cord but I blamed my decision to labor at a birthing home instead of a hospital where we could monitor his every heartbeat. If we had monitors on him, he would have survived, right?

I spent a lot of time on the floor in my son's room crying out to God the first few months. I screamed at Him. I may or may not have scared my neighbors. But this is honestly the best thing I did in the thickest of my grief. I turned to Him with every emotion and every question. I searched His Word for answers. I needed answers. I had to understand why this happened. I needed something to cling to.

God revealed Himself to me the next several months, through His Word. I began to read the Bible in a way that I had never read it before. John 3:16 says, "For God so loved the world, that he gave his only Son, that whoever believes in him should not perish but have eternal life." His one and only Son, Jesus, died. God and I have something in common. We both know what it feels like when our only son dies. He understands this pain, and He cries with us. But here's what we don't have in common: He *gave* His only Son. He *chose* for His Son to die. And it was then that I was gently reminded that His ways are higher than mine. His love for us is so great that He would sacrifice His only Son for us. That is a love far greater and higher than my comprehension.

A fellow Hope Mom said something that has stuck with me ever since. She said, "Our God is the same God that He was before our babies died." I believed He was good (or so I thought I did before Jaxon died), but I wasn't really sure *why* I believed He was good. So I began to search out His character even more. He is the same God that said, "In this world you will have trouble. But take heart! I have overcome the world" (John 16:33 NIV). Jesus conquered death when He died on the cross. Because of His Son, God promises us an eternity with our babies! The hope we find in Him is so much sweeter knowing that we will see our babies again, isn't it?

He is also the same God that has all of our days written in His book before one of them ever came to be (Psalm 139:16).

Jaxon's life was already written in His book. It was through these words that I began to let go of the sweet illusion of control that I thought I had over Jaxon's life. I loosened the claws of guilt the Devil had sunk so deep within my flesh and threw them out with the trash where they belong. If Jaxon's life had ninety years' or ten years' worth of days written in God's book, then he would be here, whether we labored in the hospital or in the street. When I began to realize this, it was so freeing!

I had a miscarriage a year later in November 2014. One more time, we mourned a life we would never get to meet on this side of heaven. But this time around, my foundation has been strong. I know my God; I don't just know *of* Him because of what others have told me. I don't know why He designed my two babies for heaven, but I do know He loves them and He loves me beyond comprehension.

I am thankful for a God who makes beauty out of ashes and redeems our pain in unexpected and wondrous ways. I thank Him for never changing so I can have this mighty thing they call an anchor for my soul. He can handle our outbursts, our confusion, and our anger. Yes, He has the power to rid this world of suffering, but we must also remember that there is so much more to His mighty plan for this sin-infected world that our brains just cannot comprehend. I thank God for teaching me how to trust Him in *all* things. I miss my Jaxon and his little sibling so much, and because of them, that sweet day will be so much sweeter!

by Michelle Garza, Hope Mom to Jaxon and Baby Garza

CHAPTER 3

WRESTLING WITH DISAPPOINTMENT, DOUBT, AND FEAR

Even though I walk through the valley
of the shadow of death,
I will fear no evil, for you are with me;
your rod and your staff, they comfort me.
—Psalm 23:4

In the days following Gwendolyn's heaven-going, I was often told, "It's okay to be angry, Erin. It's okay to yell at God." To be honest, I'm not actually sure how "okay" it is to yell at God, but I understood their point: God is big enough to handle our heartache and emotions. But it wasn't anger that was primary in my soul; it was heartache. God broke my heart, and I didn't know what to do with a shattering that profound.

Until the moment when my daughter's precious heart failed to beat, I had a relatively easy and suffering-free life. I loved God, obeyed His Word to the best of my ability, was active in a local church, was working in Christian ministry, and planned to raise my children in a way that would honor God. Because I was doing what I considered to be the "right things," I had assumed that a soul stretching of that magnitude was not going to happen to me. I was supposed to experience His blessings, not His refining discipline.

Doubt began to replace the faith I thought I had. And doubt, I learned, produces fear. My thoughts took shape like this: *Maybe I don't know God like I thought. Maybe God isn't as good as He seems. Maybe His plans for me don't actually involve good. Maybe I can't trust Him.* That kind of doubt creates a deep anxiety—if God can't be trusted, then everything is transient. Everything can be stripped away. I was familiar with the biblical story of Job—would God remove everything from me now? I would lie in bed while listening to my husband's breathing, worried that it would stop and he would slip away too.

Have you ever been to Carlsbad Caverns in southern New Mexico? It's one of the largest caves in the world, with 120 miles of mapped passages and a depth of 1,600 feet.[4] Without the artificial lighting guiding the way, you would literally be swallowed in darkness as you descended into the earth. The anxiety you experience when you are in pitch black—that's doubt leading to fear. You're unsure if you're safe; you don't know if moving would be safe; you fear the noises, the darkness, and the uncertainty.

It's not surprising that grief causes doubt, and doubt, fear. We have been plunged into the dark unknown, and the God who seemed safe and so close to us before seems nowhere to be found. We doubt His presence, His character, and His actions. You and I are not the only persons to have experienced this—the Bible is full of individuals who have walked through shadows and wondered about God's mercy. Let's study their experience and responses.

How long, O LORD? Will you forget me forever?
How long will you hide your face from me?
How long must I take counsel in my soul
and have sorrow in my heart all the day?
How long shall my enemy be exalted over me?
Consider and answer me, O LORD my God;
light up my eyes, lest I sleep the sleep of death,
lest my enemy say, "I have prevailed over him,"
lest my foes rejoice because I am shaken.
—Psalm 13:1-4

We don't know the backstory to this poem, but what emotions is the psalmist David experiencing?

What can you infer about the relationship between David and God from David's choice of words and tone?

This is an emotional reaction to what David is experiencing. It does not literally mean that God has forgotten David but that David feels so isolated that it must be as though God has forgotten him. Can you relate this this reaction?

> But I have trusted in your steadfast love;
> my heart shall rejoice in your salvation.
> I will sing to the Lord,
> because he has dealt bountifully with me.
> — Psalm 13:5-6

David ends this poetic cry with these words. What do they indicate about his faith?

What does David cling to, even while experiencing the emotional turmoil depicted in the previous verses?

> I am the man who has seen affliction
> under the rod of his [God's] wrath;
> he has driven and brought me
> into darkness without any light;
> surely against me he turns his hand
> again and again the whole day long.
> —Lamentations 3:1–3

Jeremiah the prophet is believed to be the author of Lamentations, and he wrote this lament after the destruction of Jerusalem in 586 BC.[5] How does he describe his anguish?

What is his emotional reaction to God in these verses?

> My soul is bereft of peace;
> I have forgotten what happiness is;
> so I say, "My endurance has perished;
> so has my hope from the LORD."
> Remember my affliction and my wanderings,
> the wormwood and the gall!
> My soul continually remembers it
> and is bowed down within me.
> —Lamentations 3:17–20

What does it mean to be "bereft"?

Using your own words, rephrase the author's lament in this passage.

> But this I call to mind,
> and therefore I have hope:
> The steadfast love of the LORD never ceases;
> his mercies never come to an end;
> they are new every morning;
> great is your faithfulness.
> "The LORD is my portion," says my soul,
> "therefore I will hope in him."
> The LORD is good to those who wait for him,
> to the soul who seeks him.
> It is good that one should wait quietly
> for the salvation of the LORD.
> —Lamentations 3:21–26

In verse 18, the author states that he felt his hope was gone, and in verse 21, he states that he does have hope. What caused the change?

How does the author describe God's character in this passage?

What never changes about the Lord? (Hint: see verse 22.)

For the Lord will not
cast off forever,
but, though he cause grief, he will have compassion
according to the abundance of his steadfast love;
for he does not willingly afflict
or grieve the children of men.
—Lamentations 3:31–33

What does the author believe about God's character in this passage?

In both of these passages, the authors were experiencing heavy, traumatic grief and isolation. They both felt overwhelmed, alone, and doubtful. As they poured out their heart, it paints a pretty dark picture of God and His involvement, doesn't it? And that's why it is so important to remember that emotions in themselves are not authoritative. They can come and go, and while they are valid and real, they cannot be our guide for our faith or decisions.

Both David and the author of Lamentations understood this. That is why they called to mind what they knew to be true—they chose to meditate on what they could absolutely count on. They chose to trust in the dark what had been revealed to them in the light—that God's steadfast love, mercy, and presence would uphold them. They didn't *feel* that way, but despite all their feelings, they chose to believe in God's past actions and mercy toward them.

Our key verse from Psalm 23 is a great visual picture of God's guidance *through* the valley of the shadow of death, or the "valley of deep darkness." Even though we're journeying *through* shadows (not around), and all we see and feel is darkness, we can trust and rely on the Lord, our Shepherd who leads us.

Father, it is so difficult to feel broken by You. It feels isolating and causes so much doubt and fear to surface. Would You please graciously carry us through these turbulent emotions and hold us fast? Thank You that You are "big enough for our emotions." You are so much bigger, with a vision that is higher than the fog of our grief. Would You enable us to trust You in the darkness, even as we walk in the shadow of death, waiting for Your light to shine once more? Amen.

REFLECTIONS

What emotions do you feel toward God now?

Which of these passages resonated with you and why?

Like David and Jeremiah, are you able to call the truth to mind and stand on it even when your emotions are so different? Why or why not?

GOING DEEPER:

Write your own lament to the Lord. It doesn't have to be eloquent, metered, or perfectly rhyme. Just allow your heart to cry out to Him.

HOLDEN'S STORY

I smiled at the lady staring at my round belly while waiting in line with me in the McDonald's bathroom. She asked me when I was due, and I giddily replied that I was actually on my way to the hospital in labor. (Our hospital was one and a half hours away, so of course I had to stop to use the bathroom halfway there—since my sweet boy was sitting on my bladder.) I was so glad she asked because I had to share the news with *someone*! Being a first-time mom, I did not know if I was in "real" labor, so we had not yet told our families, as they all lived several hours away and we did not want to make them hurry for nothing.

We drove up to the hospital in complete "first-time parent bliss." I wanted to remember and document each moment of our firstborn's entry into the world, and since contractions were bearable, I made my husband take photos of us outside of the hospital.

Hand in hand, we excitedly entered the hospital. I was not afraid of labor. I was too happy to meet my son to even have nerves at this point. I joked with the admissions nurse that the gowns were not made for smaller-framed girls and that they should look into cuter ones. Our room faced a sweet little pond. Everything seemed like the perfect day for my son's birthday.

They hooked me up to the fetal monitor. Silence. Our nurse told me they probably had a defective monitor and that she would be right back with a new one. I remained clueless and cheerful. At this point, I think my husband had called some family, since I was clearly in real labor. When our nurse placed the second Doppler over our baby, her face silenced us. *Certainly our little guy is just hiding. I felt him move just hours earlier.* I did not even let the worst enter my mind. The charge nurse was called; still no heartbeat. Something was terribly wrong. But he would be okay. Right? *Right?* I was pleading with our nurse. Chet was praying and crying—both of which he never does in public. In seconds, the room was filled with nurses, a specialist, and our doctor who happened to be on shift that Saturday morning.

An ultrasound confirmed our worst fears.

That moment, my world stopped. I remember physically feeling my heart burst; I truly felt like I was broken. Every part of me begged for this to be a nightmare. I was pleading with God in a way I had never done before. *Please, God, if ever there was a miracle to perform,* please *let this be it.*

This doesn't happen to healthy people.

This doesn't happen in the United States.

Our son is wanted. He is loved. He was planned.

He was talked to and prayed over every day. He has a nursery waiting for him.

This cannot really be happening to us. What did I do wrong?

God, do You hate me?

I could barely breathe; they placed an oxygen mask over my head, and my mind grew fuzzy. Our specialist took my hand and Chet's and prayed over us. A calm came over me—peace that passed my understanding, peace only the Lord can give. He thanked Jesus for our son, Holden, by name. He thanked Jesus for our son's life and purpose. The whole room was thanking Jesus for Holden and crying with us.

My mind jumped ahead to laboring and delivering a dead baby. I could not do this. Why wouldn't they just let me have a C-section? For the first time all day, I realized my contractions *really* hurt, and I had no reason to look forward to them now. I just wanted this to be over. Our doctors explained my options, and thankfully my husband was clearer minded than I was and convinced me to birth our son naturally.

I labored through prayers. On the day that held the greatest pain in my life, I had never felt so loved. Friends and family carried us through their prayers. A thoughtful nurse had called all the people on our phones' favorites lists, and unbeknownst to us, the waiting room was filled with church friends and family praying for us that whole day.

Eight hours later, Holden Newell Erwin, our precious seven-pound, five-ounce son, entered this world. Though I had never stopped begging God for him to take a miraculous breath, that was not what happened.

Holden's life has meaning and purpose beyond the dreams we had for him. Psalm 139:16 became a precious verse to us. "Your eyes saw my unformed substance; in your book were written, every one of them, the days that were formed for me, when as yet there were none of them." God knew each moment of Holden's life, and before the world was created, He knew Holden would never take a breath on this side of eternity. Little did we know how much Holden's life would change ours.

We arrived home the next day. We made decisions I never imagined having to make regarding burying our child. We laid our son's little body to rest. We performed the daily tasks needed to survive and exist, though most days I felt like all I was doing was existing. My swollen belly, the empty nursery, the incessant baby shower invites—*everything* was a reminder that my plans were crushed. Life after a stillborn often did not feel like life—or at least a life I wanted to live. I was angry with God for not giving me my son. I was angry with myself, certain that I had made some wrong decision during my pregnancy that had harmed my son. Even though I trusted God, that trust hurt. I asked why a thousand times a day.

After the raw pain of those early weeks and months subsided, I started to see the purpose in Holden's life. I grasped the beauty that God was creating through the ashes. His short life on earth was nothing compared to the eternity he has in heaven, and that truth alone (I chose Psalm 21:6 as his life verse) gave me peace. Before losing Holden, my life was comfortable; it had never *truly* been rocked to the core. I was my own life preserver. After Holden, I understood just how feeble I was and that I needed to be anchored to Christ. I had to hold on to the hope of His promises. I did not have a child in my arms to love and care for, but God opened my eyes to see so many others who needed love on earth. My husband and I were given the overwhelmingly humbling position to help carry out a clean water ministry in our son's honor. My broken heart was being mended through loving others. I had a purpose and cause to give his life a legacy here, one that honored and glorified our son's Savior.

God brought beautiful women into my life, women who also had to say good-bye to their babies. It was through their lives and stories that I felt a sense of community and lost the feeling of alienating loneliness. My Hope Mom friends were vital in my healing, as they tenderly urged me to know God deeper through grief and gave my tears a home.

Holden's story did not end on August 28, 2010, nor did my life. I could never have imagined what God had in store for our family. Though not a day has gone by that I do not miss my son, though not one milestone date has passed when I do not dream of what it would be like with Holden here with us, joy *has* replaced my grief. A Hope Mom told me shortly after we lost Holden that she could think about her hope daughter with joy in her heart. I thought she was crazy, and *knew* that day would never come for me. However, God did replace my sorrow with comfort and joy.

I smile when I tell Holden's little sisters about their big brother. Even though we knew we were not guaranteed babies after a loss, my husband and I were given the dear opportunity to be parents on this earth. Holden's first little sister was born on World Water Day in 2012. (God is in the details!) We adopted Holden's second baby sister through a Hope Mom connection a year and a half later. (Again, God is in the details.) If Holden's life had been any different, we would not have the two beautiful girls we get to call daughters today. He is good, and His plans are perfect.

First Peter 1:3–5 says this:

> Blessed be the God and Father of our Lord
> Jesus Christ! According to his great mercy, he
> has caused us to be born again to a living hope
> through the resurrection of Jesus Christ from

the dead, to an inheritance that is imperishable, undefiled, and unfading, kept in heaven for you, who by God's power are being guarded through faith for a salvation ready to be revealed in the last time.

Thank You, Jesus, for Your great mercy in giving us the gift of eternal life. God *willingly* lost His Son, so that I will get the opportunity to look into my son's eyes one day.

by Sarah Erwin, Hope Mom to Holden

CHAPTER 4

HEAVEN AND ETERNITY

 But our citizenship is in Heaven, and from it we await a Savior, the Lord Jesus Christ, who will transform our lowly body to be like his glorious body, by the power that enables him even to subject all things to himself.
—Philippians 3:20–21

In a Barna Group research study from 2003, 64 percent of Americans believe that they will go to heaven.[6] What people actually think about the nature and existence of heaven varies. It wasn't until Gwendolyn's precious physical body ceased to breathe that I began to seriously contemplate the nature of heaven. I had to know if she was real, if she went "somewhere", what she was doing, and—most importantly to my grieving heart—if I would see her again.

I began to search the Bible for the answers. After all, God is the one who created heaven; He is the authority about its nature, its occupants, and its acceptance rate. What I found was so encouraging, and it rooted my aching heart in hope.

Our children have avoided all that is bad and evil in the world and have received everything that is forever good. Being in God's presence and experiencing His goodness is so much higher and better than any earthly experience this world has to offer. We may be missing experiences for them (like growing up, getting married, having children, etc.), but they are not. Our children have been given total and complete goodness from God.

I'm praying that this chapter will open your eyes to the truth about eternity and heaven and what we have to look forward to!

ENGAGING TRUTH

The Bible teaches that there is a present (intermediate) heaven and a future heaven. The present heaven is where those who have trusted in Jesus Christ as their Savior go after they physically pass away. The future heaven is what will come after Christ returns, and God establishes the new heavens and new earth.

Present Heaven

> And he said, "Jesus, remember me when you come into your kingdom." And he said to him, "Truly, I say to you, today you will be with me in Paradise."
> —Luke 23:42–43

The thief and Jesus were moments from their physical death. What assurance did Christ give to the repentant sinner?

The Greek word for *paradise* is *pairidaeza*, which means "a walled park or enclosed garden." In Randy Alcorn's book *Heaven*, he explains.

> Paradise was not generally understood as mere allegory, with a metaphorical or spiritual meaning, but as an actual physical place where God and his people lived together, surrounded by physical beauty, enjoying great pleasures and happiness.[7]

What can we infer about the nature of the present heaven from this?

For to me to live is Christ, and to die is gain. If I am to live in the flesh, that means fruitful labor for me. Yet which I shall choose I cannot tell. I am hard pressed between the two. My desire is to depart and be with Christ, for that is far better.
—Philippians 1:21–23

How does the author, the apostle Paul, describe death?

Why would Paul be "hard pressed" when it comes to death?

Babies in Heaven

> But when David saw that his servants were whispering together,
> David understood that the child was dead. And David said to
> his servants, "Is the child dead?" They said, "He is dead." Then
> David arose from the earth and washed and anointed himself and
> changed his clothes. And he went into the house of the Lord and
> worshiped. He then went to his own house. And when he asked,
> they set food before him, and he ate. Then his servants said to him,
> "What is this thing that you have done? You fasted and wept for the
> child while he was alive; but when the child died, you arose and ate
> food." He said, "While the child was still alive, I fasted and wept, for
> I said, 'Who knows whether the Lord will be gracious to me, that the
> child may live?' But now he is dead. Why should I fast? Can I bring
> him back again? I shall go to him, but he will not return to me."
> —2 Samuel 12:19–23

King David recognizes the agonizing separation of losing a child here on earth. But what is his hope?

David was fully convinced that his son was with the Lord, and that he would see him again.[8] Compare his actions from when the child was sick to when he learned of his son's death.

Where is the first place David went after learning his son had died?

Why do you think that worship and being in the Lord's presence were of utmost importance to David?

Future Heaven

The Bible teaches that in the ultimate (future) heaven, God will come down from His place to live with us in our place, the new earth.[9]

> For behold, I create new heavens
> and a new earth,
> and the former things shall not be remembered
> or come into mind.
> —Isaiah 65:17

> But according to his promise we are waiting for new heavens and a new earth in which righteousness dwells.
> —2 Peter 3:13

What are we waiting for?

There will not be a brand-new earth; there will be a renewed earth. An earth without death, disease, decay, global warming, wars, or mosquitos.[10] What does Peter tell us will dwell in the new earth?

And I saw the holy city, new Jerusalem, coming down out of heaven from God, prepared as a bride adorned for her husband. And I heard a loud voice from the throne saying, "Behold, the dwelling place of God is with man. He will dwell with them, and they will be his people, and God himself will be with them as their God. He will wipe away every tear from their eyes, and death shall be no more, neither shall there be mourning nor crying nor pain anymore, for the former things have passed away."
—Revelation 21:2–4

Where will God dwell?

What does God promise will come to an end?

They shall build houses and inhabit them;
they shall plant vineyards and eat their fruit.
They shall not build and another inhabit;
they shall not plant and another eat;
for like the days of a tree shall the days of my people be,
and my chosen shall long enjoy the work of their hands.
—Isaiah 65:21–22

Summarize the depictions of eternal life for Christians.

Learning more about what heaven and eternity will contain has been so beneficial for me on an everyday basis. I can look forward to heaven because I've learned more about its realities and the joy I will have when I am there. I am confident that I will see my daughter again, and I am so grateful that the Bible gives us this assurance.

On a final note about our babies in heaven, I know it's a common idea that children become angels after they die. It may be sweet to call a baby "a little angel," but it's not accurate or realistic. It's much more honoring to them and obedient to God to refer to them as what they are: beloved children in the sight of Christ. Please see appendix A for more detailed information.

Thank You, Christ, for accomplishing what we could never do—for opening a way to God and giving us the hope of heaven. Would You build in us such joy and anticipation as we look forward to the day when we see You face-to-face? Amen.

REFLECTIONS

What ideas have you had about heaven that may be contrary to what you just studied above?

As you think about heaven, what gives you comfort?

Why do people think that babies become angels?

GOING DEEPER:

Write a letter to your little one, and share with him or her the hope you have of seeing one day what he or she is currently seeing and experiencing.

BROOKLYN'S STORY

On November 14, 2012, I became a mom for the first time. My daughter Brooklyn was born after an emotionally difficult pregnancy. At twenty weeks' gestation, my husband and I were told Brooklyn had a heart defect that would likely require surgery within the first six months of her life. So we anticipated hardship. We anticipated a difficult first few months for Brooklyn's life. But there was hope that we would see it through. A difficult life, a challenging life, was still a life, and we were scared but grateful.

The first twenty-four hours after Brooklyn was born, more complications presented themselves in her little four-pound body. On her seventh day on earth, we were told there might not be many more. Brooklyn was knit together with a lethal genetic disorder called trisomy 18. Most babies with trisomy 18 are miscarried or stillborn, and many don't live past the second week of life. Our hearts had never known such devastation, such heartbreak. We were grasping for any past experience, any skill set we'd developed, any "tool" to help us navigate our way down this scary road we were being led down, but we came up empty. We were not prepared for anything other than a *happily ever after*. We weren't even given the hope of that. We were, quite literally, given a death sentence.

What we knew changed everything. It had to. Each and every moment we had with Brooklyn became a gift. The mundane acts of caring for her became sacred and cherished. Small accomplishments, like gaining weight and making eye contact, became major victories worthy of celebration. Sometimes, these feelings of thankfulness and celebration came easily, and sometimes, they were a struggle. Often, it felt easier to sink into despair at the thought of the difficult days ahead without our sweet girl.

These moments with Brooklyn accumulated to days, weeks, and months. On March 13, 2013, our odds-defying firstborn baby girl went to be with Jesus. Though in those last moments of holding her tiny body, I didn't give much thought to where she was going. I just wanted her to stay here with us. But the reality was I couldn't keep her. She was destined for eternity, and that was a reality I wasn't prepared to face.

In the days and weeks following Brooklyn's death, I wrestled with the idea of eternity. Did it really exist? Was there really a place that her spirit went to? All the things I had learned in my Christian school and Sunday school education didn't feel like enough to satisfy the unrest in my heart.

During Brooklyn's short life, I always knew where she was. When she wasn't in my arms, I knew the distance between us—whether that was a few feet away in the Pack 'n Play or the next room in her crib. But when she died, I felt so unhinged, not knowing where she was. I mean I knew physically where she *was*, but was she really more than a lifeless body? More than ashes? Did she truly exist somewhere else? And if so, would I ever be reunited with her?

There was certainly a large component of revisiting the truths I had been taught. I spent time reading what the Bible and people who had studied the Bible had to say about the reality of eternity, but I also began to cry out to God for answers, for any kind of assurance that I would see Brooklyn again. But these questions were often met with more questions, including these:

"Even if I don't get to see Brooklyn again, can I still trust Him? Will He still be enough?"

Living in this tender place led to moments of spiritual anguish and pain that I honestly don't like to think about, but what I call to mind, and often do, is the comfort I received from Him in these low moments. Sometimes, it was words of truth; sometimes, it was a mental picture; sometimes, it was a conversation with a friend; but each time, I knew it was from Him because of the peace and rest He left behind. And in all of this, I began to trust that He was near.

As this new trust in the Lord was being strengthened, it became easier to trust in the reality of eternity. But as with any new truth your spirit grabs ahold of, I needed to learn what that meant for me in my present moments. Throughout my day, I thought about Brooklyn all the time. I wondered what heaven might be like. What might she be doing? What did she look like now? It taught me how to be mindful of eternity in a new way—in a very real way. It was no longer a theory but a truth that impacted the way I thought and lived. When I was going for a morning run, Brooklyn was with her Father, the angels, and the saints in heaven. When I was at the grocery store, she was in glory. I needed to practice believing that in this present moment, I exist, she exists, and He exists. Eternity isn't so far off. Brooklyn isn't so far off. The Lord Himself is not far off.

If you were to scroll through my Instagram account during the time when Brooklyn was with us, you'd find pictures of a really cute baby, and most of them were taken next to a chalkboard with a number written on it. We considered every day we had with her to be a gift, so we kept careful count of each one. Knowing this number was limited made every day something to be thankful for and worthy of celebration.

Before Brooklyn, the fact that my days on earth were limited didn't really hit home. Life seemed like it would go on forever, and if I'm honest, I didn't have a real interest in going to heaven. The stuff I'd pictured of angels, people in white robes, and a never-ending church service was not compelling to me. At different stages of life, I remember feeling sad when I thought about the possibility of dying before I got to do or experience that coveted thing. At sixteen, it was getting my license. In college, it was getting married. When I got married, it was having kids. Now, after experiencing the brokenness of this world through my daughter's broken body, I would leave it all behind in an instant. When the grief was new, this desire to be done with this earthly life stemmed from my ache to be with Brooklyn again, but the farther along I walked the road of grief, the more I sought and experienced comfort and healing from the only One who can truly give it. This vulnerable journey toward healing allowed me to see the true prize. I still long for the day when I will be reunited with my daughter, but I long even more to be with the One who has walked so closely with me in my pain. He willingly gave His life because He eternally loves me—me and Brooklyn.

What I know deep in my heart about the truth of eternity, and the one who won it for me, has changed everything. It had to! Sitting around the dinner table with friends and family has become more sacred. Doing housework or yard work has been infused with purpose. My moments have become more special because they simply, are. And because they have profound meaning for this life and the one to come. At the very same time, the hardship and struggle I face has an end. Hallelujah! When I'm in the middle of the same argument I keep having over and over with my husband, or facing another disappointment, or another heartbreak, it can lighten the heavy load to remind myself that one day these struggles will be over and my tears will be wiped away forever. I will live in perfect peace, in a perfect world, with my Creator. This hope finds me in all circumstances, all shifting feelings, and calls me back to a place I haven't yet seen but I know my heart, and Brooklyn's heart, was made for.

by Corrie Hull, Hope Mom to Brooklyn

CHAPTER 5

BIBLICAL MOURNING IS ROOTED IN HOPE

 But we do not want you to be uninformed, brothers, about those who are asleep, that you may not grieve as others do who have no hope.
—1 Thessalonians 4:13

The word *hope*, defined by dictionary.com, is "To look forward to with desire and reasonable confidence."[11] Biblical hope is certain and reliable because it is founded upon the One who is certain and reliable. It takes hold of God and His promises and cements itself into God's unchanging goodness.

Hope is obviously a big thing to us here at Hope Mommies. In part, the ministry actually began as an alternative to being called "Angel Mommies" or "Baby Loss Mommies." As we learned in the past chapter, our children are not angels, and they are not lost! Our babies were "born out of hope, prayed for in hope, taken to Christ in hope."[12]

We are Hope Mommies.

And yet we mourn. And that is okay.

As each of you know, grief does deep, unexplainable things to your body, mind, and soul. I'm not a doctor or psychologist, so I won't try to delve into those areas. What I do know is that the Bible is not silent about grief and mourning. It speaks, encourages, and instructs, and in this chapter, we will be talking about how those who are of the family of God grieve with hope.

I'm praying that as you study, this will be a time of crying out to God and hearing His response to you. His ability to save is not weakened; His ear is not deaf to the cries of His children. The cross is not too small for the enormity of your grief. God did not leave us in a broken world without offering hope. Without God's intervention into the fractured story of mankind, there would be little to look forward to.

We're going to study four ways that God's Word gives hope and redemption.

ENGAGING TRUTH

Hope That God Offers: Salvation

> But your iniquities have made a separation
> between you and your God,
> and your sins have hidden his face from you
> so that he does not hear.
> —Isaiah 59:2

Why are we separated from God?

> If we confess our sins, he is faithful and just to forgive us our sins
> and to cleanse us from all unrighteousness.
> —1 John 1:9

Why must we be cleansed?

Who has the authority and power to forgive sins?

What must we do to receive forgiveness? Have you done this?

Hope That God Offers: Sustaining Faith

The Lord upholds all who are falling
and raises up all who are bowed down.
—Psalm 145:14

My flesh and my heart may fail,
but God is the strength of my heart and my portion forever.
—Psalm 73:26

What will the Lord do for His children who are disheartened or broken?

What is God's commitment to and provision for His children?

Hope That God Offers: Seeing Our Babies Again

> For this we declare to you by a word from the Lord, that we
> who are alive, who are left until the coming of the Lord, will not
> precede those who have fallen asleep. For the Lord himself will
> descend from heaven with a cry of command, with the voice of an
> archangel, and with the sound of the trumpet of God. And the
> dead in Christ will rise first. Then we who are alive, who are left, will
> be caught up together with them in the clouds to meet the Lord in
> the air, and so we will always be with the Lord. Therefore encourage
> one another with these words.
> —1 Thessalonians 4:15–18

Who will rise from the dead? (Hint: see verse 16.)

When will we be united with our children again?

What is this passage meant to do?

Hope That God Offers: Comfort through a Personal Relationship with God through Jesus Christ

> Give ear to my words, O LORD;
> consider my groaning.
> Give attention to the sound of my cry,
> my King and my God,
> for to you do I pray.
> O LORD, in the morning you hear my voice;
> in the morning I prepare a sacrifice for you and watch.
> —Psalm 5:1–3

To whom does the psalmist cry out? _____

> I love you, O LORD, my strength.
> The LORD is my rock and my fortress and my deliverer,
> my God, my rock, in whom I take refuge,
> my shield, and the horn of my salvation, my stronghold.

I call upon the LORD, who is worthy to be praised,
and I am saved from my enemies.
The cords of death encompassed me;
the torrents of destruction assailed me;
the cords of Sheol entangled me;
the snares of death confronted me.
In my distress I called upon the LORD;
to my God I cried for help.
From his temple he heard my voice,
and my cry to him reached his ears.
—Psalm 18:1–6

When did the psalmist call upon the Lord?

Was his cry heard?

What does it mean for God to be a "stronghold" in times of distress?

He sent from on high, he took me;
he drew me out of many waters.
He rescued me from my strong enemy
and from those who hated me,
for they were too mighty for me.
They confronted me in the day of my calamity,
but the LORD was my support.
He brought me out into a broad place;
he rescued me, because he delighted in me.
—Psalm 18:16–19

What verbs are used in this section to describe God's actions?

Why did God rescue him?

Out of the depths I cry to you, O Lord!
O Lord, hear my voice!
Let your ears be attentive
to the voice of my pleas for mercy!
If you, O Lord, should mark iniquities,
O Lord, who could stand?
But with you there is forgiveness,
that you may be feared.
I wait for the Lord, my soul waits,
and in his word I hope;
my soul waits for the Lord
more than watchmen for the morning,
more than watchmen for the morning.
O Israel, hope in the Lord!
For with the Lord there is steadfast love,
and with him is plentiful redemption.
And he will redeem Israel
from all his iniquities.
—Psalm 130

What two things does the psalmist do?

Why does the psalmist believe he will be heard?

God is not taken aback by your intense mourning. It's not unspiritual to grieve. Death is an enemy and intruder and will only be completely eradicated when Christ returns (1 Corinthians 15:26). When you read through the Bible, you find examples of prolonged periods of mourning—it was good and right to acknowledge the severity of a life cut short. We were made for endless life with God and each other, and anything less than that is grievous. Yet, praise God, He gives us hope! We can have confidence that if we've repented and believed in Christ for salvation, we will go to heaven; if we're His children, He will hear us and answer us; and He will give us His Spirit to sustain us while we wait.

Thank You, Abba, that You did not leave us as orphans—unloved, without protection, hope, or a future. Instead, You have given us all of those things through Christ Jesus. Would You strengthen our hope and secure it to the cross where You displayed Your faithfulness toward those who previously rejected You? Enable this dear sister to grieve her loss with hope. Amen.

REFLECTIONS

Psalm 18 describes God as a rock of refuge when the psalmist was in distress. How would you describe your relationship with God today?

Has your grief been rooted in hope? Why or why not? What is it rooted in?

If you were to die today, where would you be and why?

GOING DEEPER:

Give your heart room to grieve this week. Go on a walk with a friend and talk about how you're mourning. Or listen aloud to the psalms and write out your response.

SIMEON'S STORY

It was the beginning of my fourteenth week of pregnancy when I went in for a routine ultrasound and prenatal appointment. I had been eagerly looking forward to this day for many weeks. Those fourteen weeks seemed to pass by painfully slow as I waited for our scheduled appointment. It seemed so strange to be this far along in our pregnancy without having yet seen this precious life forming inside me. I'm still not even sure why I was not able to get an appointment to see our midwife for the entire first trimester, but it was a difficult wait! The previous few days had been really busy for our family, so my husband decided last minute to stay home with our boys while I drove off with our three-year-old daughter to finally see this smallest addition to our family.

On our way to the appointment, my daughter squealed, "Mommy! I am so excited to see our baby!" As those words left her little mouth, a giant pit formed in my stomach, and suddenly I felt all sorts of anxiety. Something just didn't seem right anymore. I tried to shake off that feeling, reminding myself that I was fourteen weeks along and had never experienced any symptoms of a possible problem. Surely, we were in the clear! Still, I spent the entire drive fighting back nervous tears and asking God to fill my anxious heart with His perfect peace.

We arrived at the doctor's office and were almost immediately called back for my ultrasound. As the first glimpse of our little one appeared on the monitor, my mommy heart knew that something was not right. He was not as big as I had expected for a baby who had completed its first trimester of development. And he was completely still. It hadn't taken me very long to realize that Schmidt babies are never still.

After a few moments of searching, our ultrasonographer confirmed what I already knew to be true. Our baby's heart was not beating. And mine was aching. I looked over at my daughter, who was sitting in the chair next to me. She was beaming. Completely unaware of what the ultrasonographer had said, she was watching the screen. She knew she was looking at her baby and she could not have been more proud! A pit formed in my stomach for the second time that morning as I called her over to sit on my lap and explained to her that our baby's heart was not working and that God had decided to take the baby to be with Him in heaven.

Tears formed in her tender eyes as she said, "Oh, I am so sad that our baby's heart is not working because we will really miss our baby." Then she paused, cupped my chin with her sweet hands, and said thoughtfully, "But aren't you glad that God has let me be with you for so many days?" What a precious glimpse of God's grace through the eyes of that wonderfully dear girl. I didn't think I would ever be able to stop hugging that her.

I was moved into another room to wait to meet with other nurses and doctors who would tell me what to expect in the coming days and weeks. As I sat in the silence waiting for the first nurse to arrive, and trying to find the words to tell my husband what had happened, I could hear from the room next to mine the sound that I had been longing to hear just a few minutes before. It sounded like horses galloping under water—the sound of a tiny heart beating from inside its mother's womb. But it was not the heart of my little one. My eyes filled with tears. Oh, how I wanted him here with me!

The midwife came in, tears in her own eyes, as she explained what my options were. I could either schedule a D&C to have the pregnancy removed right away or I could wait for my body to recognize our loss and miscarry naturally. My heart felt like it was being twisted up tight as I thought about having our sweet baby removed from my body in the same way that an unwanted baby was removed during an abortion. I just couldn't do that. I wanted that baby! I wanted him with the entirety of my heart. I was sure I was going to get sick right there in the exam room at the thought. Choking back that nauseous feeling, I told her I would wait and allow my body to miscarry on its own.

Before my appointment was complete, I asked my midwife for our ultrasound picture. Everyone was surprised by my request. I guess they figured that I would want to put this day behind me. But even though our little one's life on earth was so short, God gave him to us. He chose to add him to our family. And we will never be able to put him *behind* us, because every day we are looking *ahead* to the day that we will see him again in heaven. Our best days together are yet to come.

When I finally left the doctor's office several hours after I had anticipated being there, I wept. All the way home, I wept. And when I walked in the house and sat down on the couch next to my husband, we both wept together. From the very first moment that we found out that God had begun new life inside me, that sweet baby was deeply loved. I was due just a few days before our daughter's fourth birthday, and we couldn't have been more excited. We firmly believe that children are a blessing from the Lord, and through that little life, God has blessed us beyond what we ever believed possible.

With grateful, joyful hearts, we celebrated the news of our pregnancy with family and friends. And with heavy hearts, just a few months later, we mourned as we shared the news of his death.

I thought about the picture I had taken just a few weeks earlier of our kids holding the positive pregnancy test in excitement. I had planned on publicly sharing that picture right after our appointment in order to finally announce to everyone that we were expecting our fourth baby. It felt like a great loss to never be able to announce our pregnancy to the world in the way we had planned. But I realized that death did not render that picture untrue. He is still our fourth baby, and our hearts are still glad that God chose to add him to our family.

My body felt raw and numb as I thought of carrying the lifeless body of our little one inside my own. I wondered if that was why I had felt off for the past few weeks because some part of me knew that his life had been taken from this earth. Although we will never know for sure on this side of eternity what our baby's gender is, we had both thought we were having a boy and decided to name him Simeon.

Simeon. His name means, "The Lord has heard." It is a word that was used in response to a cry for help. Our hearts had been constantly crying to God for help as we journeyed through the pain of loss, and we were filled with a full assurance that God had heard us. Day after day, He continually and graciously supplied all that we needed to continue to trust in Him, His goodness, and His plan for our lives. He indeed was our peace.

During the days and weeks that followed, every time I felt a slight flutter inside me, I would picture him moving around, stretching those ever-growing limbs, only to remember that he was no longer growing, breathing, and living. And heaven seemed so far away.

The first Sunday after finding out we had lost our baby, even though hardly anyone knew we had even been pregnant, I felt like everyone could see right through me, knowing that I was no longer carrying life but death. I felt dirty, broken, and exposed. The visible signs of pregnancy were constant reminders of the loss that we suffering through. Every day I would pray, "Father God, I know that You are more than capable of restoring life to this stilled little heart, but if that is not Your plan for us, please teach me how to honor You through this loss because I can't do this without You!"

A few weeks later, my husband and I went to a follow-up appointment to determine if my body was starting to respond to the loss. We had another ultrasound to verify that our baby had stopped developing. And while it was so hard to hear the confirmed diagnosis, my husband affirmed the truth that was so evident on our daughter's face just a few weeks earlier. We were so proud of our baby! As we saw him one last time, we were honored to have been chosen as his parents.

Weeks later, there were still no signs that my body was willing to let go of this pregnancy. Because the risk of infection was now much greater, the doctor strongly recommended that I have the D&C done. At this point, even if my body naturally miscarried, there was still a good chance that it would not be able to get rid of all of the tissue, which would require that I have it surgically removed anyway.

For the next few days, I prayed and prayed and prayed. My heart felt so unsettled at the idea of going into surgery to end our pregnancy. Even though our little one was already with the Lord, I hated the thought of his little body being torn from mine. This wasn't the way I had wanted it to end. *But God.* Oh how those two words have transformed our loss. But God was faithful. But God surrounded us with caring hearts and serving hands. But God filled my aching heart with a peace beyond measure. But God was always there—every moment—through it all.

The day of my surgery arrived, and although I had not slept a minute the night before, I was covered with a calm that can only come with the Father's presence. I have never felt His presence so fully. I literally felt like I did not take a single step all day. I was being carried by the one who had also endured the death of His own precious Son.

As we continue to walk through this loss, we are learning day by day to rejoice. And as we endure, God is teaching us how to hope. Every day from the moment we found out that our child's heart had stopped beating, I have clung to the hope that our sovereign God works out every detail of our lives for His glory.

My husband and I have spent many evenings together missing our little one and letting all of the real and raw and rough bits of our hearts pour out into each other's arms. We know that we are on this road together, and each step is bringing us closer to God and each other. Even during those days when my body felt all kinds of terrible and the pain was a constant reminder that our baby was no longer with us—yes, even then—I had hope.

Hope in the God who desired to bring Simeon into existence. Hope in the God who saw fit to take him home before he had suffered in this world. Hope in the God who chose Simeon to be in His presence, giving him the very best!

My heart has been a hurricane of emotion all this time. There were days when I just couldn't seem to back away from all of the grief and pain. And others when I have been gripped by the fear that as time passes and the normalcy of life settles in around me, our child will be forgotten by others—or his life thought less significant.

But I have come to realize that the Lord has done an incredible work in my life during this time. And as hard as it is to think through all that we have endured in losing a child, I think I would do it all over again if I was given a choice.

Please hear me out. I miss our baby. Tremendously. My heart still aches every single day. And my arms have continually yearned to hold our little one on this broken earth. But my husband shared something as he was preaching on joy for the student ministry of our church that has been echoing in my heart and mind ever since then. He said, "The Lord knows that the quickest way into our hearts is through a wound."

In God's great mercy to me, the Spirit has worked in my life in such a way that I have been compelled to allow Him access into my heart through the wound caused by the loss of our baby. And since that wound was so vast, God has had an enormous door to walk through.

God has faithfully used loss to draw us closer to Himself and teach us how to love more deeply and truly than we had been capable of before. And we know that God is not done teaching us, growing us, and stretching us through that little life.

My heart rejoices that right now, my sweet baby is enjoying that Psalm 16:11 fullness of joy as he lives forever in the perfect presence of our great God! I look forward to the day when I will wrap my arms around him for the first time! When I will see him face-to-face full of life! When I will be able to tell him just how much we love him and just how much he has changed our lives and touched our hearts! Someday we will join him in God's glorious presence. But until then, we will long for heaven and treasure our little one in our hearts while living each day on this side of eternity for the glory of our God of hope.

by Ashlee Schmidt, Hope Mom to Simeon

CHAPTER 6

ENEMIES OF YOUR SOUL

 You prepare a table before me in the
presence of my enemies.
—Psalm 23:5

Have you read the book *Hinds' Feet on High Places* by Hannah Hurnard?
It's an allegorical story about the Christian life, similar to *Pilgrim's
Progress*. The main character, Much-Afraid, journeys through valleys
and mountaintops to arrive at the High Places—the place where the
Shepherd (i.e., Jesus) lives. Much-Afraid is given two companions for her
pilgrimage: Suffering and Sorrow. Along the way, Much-Afraid encounters
many enemies that try to hinder her relationship to the Shepherd and keep
her from the high places.

The characters that our heroine meets are allegorical expressions of an
emotion. Envy, Pride, Self-Pity, and Fear are a few. They were roadblocks
for her journey and caused many a detour for her. After Gwendolyn died,
I had never been so aware that I have a very real enemy—Satan—and
he hates me—my life, my marriage, and my family—all because I belong
to God. In 1 Peter 5:8, we're told that the Devil is like a roaring lion
prowling around for someone to devour. He is actively doing whatever
it takes to derail my faith in the Lord, stunt my spiritual growth, and

weaken my influence for Christ. I do not believe Satan is responsible for Gwendolyn's death; the Bible makes it clear that God alone calls people from dust to dust. But Satan was capitalizing on my heartache by sending his arrows of anger, jealousy, resentment, bitterness, self-pity, and anything else he could throw at me to kill my hope in God and keep me focused on me.

Our culture will tell us that emotions are neutral—neither good nor evil. But the Bible makes it clear that there is morality or immorality in our emotions, and our emotions lead to action (Mark 7:14–23, Luke 6:45). There is a very real Enemy who is out to destroy you, and I'm sure that he has already barbed his arrows and struck at you—in the grocery store with the mom who seems ungrateful for her children; there is anger and bitterness waiting for you on the cereal aisle. With the fact that so many women seem blissfully pregnant and easily able to conceive and give birth, envy, self-pity, and resentment are chattering away at you, trying to convince you that God isn't there and He doesn't love you.

Yet Psalm 23 says, "You prepare a table before me in the presence of my enemies." God has set a feast and invited you to refresh yourself and rest in Him. He's not denying the reality of those emotions. He recognizes the temptation they hold. Yet He promises His presence to comfort you, and His salvation from the sin they can produce.

These emotions are real. The Enemy is real. Your faith is at stake.

But God is greater. And He will rescue. I pray that as you study, the Lord will equip you to tackle these heavy emotions and find the solution to resisting them in God's Word.

ENGAGING TRUTH

A tranquil heart gives life to the flesh,
but envy makes the bones rot.
—Proverbs 14:30

How can envy affect a person?

What is the opposite effect of envy—the blessing of a "tranquil heart"?

A fool gives full vent to his spirit,
but a wise man quietly holds it back.
—Proverbs 29:11

What does it mean to give "full vent" to your spirit?

How is the person who holds back from giving free reign to his spirit described?

> For pressing milk produces curds,
> pressing the nose produces blood,
> and pressing anger produces strife.
> —Proverbs 30:33

What will happen if you allow anger to build?

Put to death therefore what is earthly in you: sexual immorality, impurity, passion, evil desire, and covetousness, which is idolatry. On account of these the wrath of God is coming. In these you too once walked, when you were living in them. But now you must put them all away: anger, wrath, malice, slander, and obscene talk from your mouth. Do not lie to one another, seeing that you have put off the old self with its practices and have put on the new self, which is being renewed in knowledge after the image of its creator.
—Colossians 3:5–10

What does this say is "earthly" (or natural) in us?

What are we to do about those desires or emotions?

What emotions or enemies do you need to personally put away?

Put on then, as God's chosen ones, holy and
beloved, compassion, kindness, humility, meekness, and patience,
bearing with one another and, if one has a complaint against
another, forgiving each other; as the Lord has forgiven you, so you
also must forgive. And above all these put on love, which binds
everything together in perfect harmony. And let the peace of Christ
rule in your hearts, to which indeed you were called in one body.
And be thankful.
—Colossians 3:12–15

What are we to "put on"?

How are we to respond when someone offends or hurts us?

It is so much easier to give in to an emotional enemy than to put it away (or, more literally, "to death"). But I hope you've seen that these enemies are not just a one-time retort or reaction. Each time we give in a little bit more to envy or bitterness or anger, we are in deep waters. We will quickly need rescuing if we ever hope to be a woman who is loving, kind, or merciful. Galatians 5:22 talks about the fruit (the result) of the Holy Spirit's work in our lives. "But the fruit of the Spirit is love, joy, peace, patience, kindness, goodness, faithfulness, gentleness, self-control; against such things there is no law." I don't know about you, but I want to be a woman who embodies those qualities. That isn't possible unless I repent, put away the evil enemies that lurk within my own heart, and allow God to transform me.

Father, we need Your help. These feelings are very real and can be very powerful. But we know that You are greater and stronger, and so we rest on Your merit. Would You please convict us quickly when an enemy is tempting us and remind us by Your Spirit, so we are able to walk in a manner worthy of You? Amen.

REFLECTIONS

What negative emotions or "enemies" from these verses do you feel the most often?

Why should we consider these enemies of our faith?

How do you respond when facing these enemies? What can you do?

GOING DEEPER:

Imagine that your story is an allegory. What enemies are you meeting on your journey? What encouraging characters have you encountered (Mercy, Patience, Grace, etc.)?

NOAH'S STORY

We stood in a circle in my living room as my dad prayed over us before sending us up the road to the hospital to meet our son. I was thirty-nine weeks and two days pregnant and scheduled for a C-section because of a small umbilical hernia that would most likely correct itself. But we wanted to be safe, so a Cesarean it was.

Upon arrival, I changed into my hospital gown, shaking from a mixture of nervousness and excitement. When the nurse started prepping me for surgery, she attached a fetal monitor to my stomach to monitor the baby. She struggled to find a heartbeat. Another nurse came in and tried, but she was also unsuccessful. They did their best to make it all seem like no big deal as they called in a doctor with an ultrasound machine, but I knew. I watched the doctor's eyes glaze over as he stared at the ultrasound screen, and I knew that he wasn't even looking anymore. There was no heartbeat … He just didn't know how to say it.

I'm pretty sure that all the doctor got out was "I'm sorry," before my world crumbled around me and I was instantly buried beneath the rubble. I always thought the way people wailed and screamed on TV was dramatic and overacted. In that moment, I learned that it's the truest reaction there is.

We decided that the best course of action would be to cancel the surgery and induce labor. Twelve hours later, at 12:53 a.m. on September 22, 2010, I gave birth to a four-pound, nine-ounce baby boy, Noah Daniel. The silence was deafening.

We held him and allowed the nurse to take a few pictures. I wish I would have known how badly I would want those photos now; I would have taken more.

I slept for a short while but woke early and wanted to spend more time with him before saying good-bye. I sat in a quiet room in the nursery and sang to him while we rocked. I prayed that God would breathe life into him and that if that was not His will, that He would breathe life into me because in my heart, I felt just as dead as my son. I never knew until that day that it is possible to physically feel your heart break.

That afternoon, we held and kissed our sweet baby's face, and then we left the hospital knowing that we would never see our son again this side of heaven.

At home, it all began to sink in as tiny clothes and diapers were packed away; I knew they would never be worn. In the depths of grief, I questioned God, full of anger and bitterness.

It wasn't fair. Why did my son die but hers lived?

How could and why would a good God allow my baby to be snatched right from his mother's womb like that?

There were babies everywhere, and life felt like one giant kick in the stomach. My heart was broken, and at times all I could feel were anger, resentment, bitterness, envy, and entitlement. But Jeremiah 17:9 says, "The heart is deceitful above all things, and desperately sick." My heart was lying to me, and Satan was capitalizing on my grief and trying to use it as a doorway to step into my life. His desire is to turn us away from God, and a grieving mother is vulnerable prey.

I knew I had a choice. I could continue to be angry and bitter, or I could trust God. For me, turning my back on God meant that my son became a statistic. We had played the baby lottery and lost. Choosing to trust God meant that my son was not a statistic but is still a purposefully and lovingly created child of God who lived and died for the glory of the Lord.

I began listening to "Desert Song" by Hillsong United daily. I sang the words "All of my life, in every season, you are still God. I have a reason to sing. I have a reason to worship" every day. Even though my heart did not feel that, I sang it and prayed it because, despite how my heart felt, I knew it was true.

I began to heal as I surrendered myself, my life, and my son to God. I began to pray, "Not my will but Yours be done."

As I opened up my hands, barren and naked at the foot of the cross, God revealed Himself to me in many profound ways and showed me His faithfulness firsthand.

And one day, a few months later, as I sang my desert song, I began to cry. Because that day, I didn't just know it. I meant it.

"Oh, taste and see that the LORD is good! Blessed
is the man who takes refuge in him!"
—Psalm 34:8

by Kelly Mahalak, Hope Mom to Noah

CHAPTER 7

GRIEVING TOGETHER

 Love bears all things, believes all things,
hopes all things, endures all things.
—1 Corinthians 13:7

Think back on your wedding day.

If you said the traditional vows, you and your glowing, love-struck spouse
may have repeated this phrase "for better or for worse, in sickness and in
health." This—this horrible tragedy and grief of losing your baby—is part of
the "worse" that you committed to loving one another through. Marriage
is not for the faint of heart, even without the burden of loss.

Knowing how to relate to your spouse in the middle of grief is one of
the most frequently discussed topics for many Hope Moms. More than
likely, you both handle emotions very differently. He may want to be busy,
while you want to sleep the day away. He may be able to laugh and joke
with friends, and you have no idea how to paint a smile on your face. Or
perhaps the opposite is true and he can't understand your seemingly
cavalier attitude.

Whatever your marriage looks like now, take heart. God is *for* your
marriage. He wants you to be moving toward Him and one another, not

apart. The Holy Spirit is the ultimate Counselor (John 16:13), and He takes an active interest in your marriage and your heart. God's Word is sufficient for all things, and He has something to say to you about your marriage.

This chapter is about *you* because you are the only person in your marriage that you can actually change. It covers the foundational truth that we must have in order for our marriages to survive loss. It's not a "Five Steps to Discuss Grief with Your Spouse" guide but a barometer for your ideals and expectations. Do you believe and accept God's design for *your* marriage? Are you ready to commit to act upon it, even when it's difficult? I pray your study is fruitful for your heart and your marriage as you read about God's beautiful plan for you through this covenant called marriage.

ENGAGING TRUTH

God's Goal for Marriage: Spiritual, Emotional, and Physical Unity and Oneness

> Then the man said,
> "This at last is bone of my bones
> and flesh of my flesh;
> she shall be called Woman,
> because she was taken out of Man."
> Therefore a man shall leave his father and his mother and hold fast
> to his wife, and they shall become one flesh.
> —Genesis 2:23–24

Fill in the blanks: "A man shall _____ his father and his mother and _____ to his wife, and they shall become _____."

God establishes the covenant of marriage at the very beginning. A covenant is an agreement meant to endure forever. Describe what those terms look like (leave, hold fast, become one flesh) in real life.

Now concerning the matters about which you wrote: "It is good for a man not to have sexual relations with a woman." But because of the temptation to sexual immorality, each man should have his own wife and each woman her own husband. The husband should give to his wife her conjugal rights, and likewise the wife to her husband. For the wife does not have authority over her own body, but the husband does. Likewise the husband does not have authority over his own body, but the wife does. Do not deprive one another, except perhaps by agreement for a limited time, that you may devote yourselves to prayer; but then come together again, so that Satan may not tempt you because of your lack of self-control.
—1 Corinthians 7:1–5

What reasons can you find in this passage that shows the importance of sexuality in the marriage covenant?

What is the acceptable reason to withhold from sexual intimacy, according to this passage? (Hint: see verse 5.)

If you must refrain from intimacy, what should you be doing instead?[13]

God's Goal for Marriage: To Mimic Christ and His bride, the Church

> Wives, submit to your own husbands, as to the Lord. For the husband is the head of the wife even as Christ is the head of the church, his body, and is himself its Savior. Now as the church submits to Christ, so also wives should submit in everything to their husbands.
>
> Husbands, love your wives, as Christ loved the church and gave himself up for her, that he might sanctify her, having cleansed her by the washing of water with the word, so that he might present the church to himself in splendor, without spot or wrinkle or any such thing, that she might be holy and without blemish. In the same way husbands should love their wives as their own bodies. He who loves his wife loves himself. For no one ever hated his own flesh, but nourishes and cherishes it, just as Christ does the church, because we are members of his body. "Therefore a man shall leave his father and mother and hold fast to his wife, and the two shall become one flesh." This mystery is profound, and I am saying that it refers to Christ and the church. However, let each one of you love his wife as himself, and let the wife see that she respects her husband.
> —Ephesians 5:22–33

How does Christ love the church?

How are submission and love reflected in the relationship between Christ and the church?

What are the commands for wives in this passage?

In your own words, what is biblical submission?[14]

God's Goal for Marriage: Reflecting God's Love toward Your Spouse

> Love is patient and kind; love does not envy or boast; it is not arrogant or rude. It does not insist on its own way; it is not irritable or resentful; it does not rejoice at wrongdoing, but rejoices with the truth. Love bears all things, believes all things, hopes all things, endures all things.
> —1 Corinthians 13:4–7

Which of these characteristics of love are you craving from your spouse? Which do you think they are craving from you?

What does love do in regard to "all things"?

You and your spouse were handpicked by God for one another. And He knew that at the beginning of your love story, this tragedy would come. Yet He *still* chose you for the other person! You are each other's best ally. It's easy to make your spouse the enemy or their action (or inaction) to be the disrupting factor of your day. Don't allow these little lies to take root. Your spouse is grieving, just as you are. And even if they are not responding to you or to God in a way that is right, you are still responsible for your part of this covenant. Is your heart committed to God's goals for your marriage?

Abba, You designed marriage to reflect Your incredible faithfulness, unity, and sacrifice. Would You please enable us to love our spouses in a way that honors and glorifies You? Give us eyes to see where we have wronged them and humble hearts to seek forgiveness. Bind our hearts to our spouse to serve, love, and grieve with hope in a way that strengthens our marriage covenant. Amen.

REFLECTIONS

Review God's goals for marriage from this chapter. Which is the most difficult for you in your marriage right now and why?

How have you grieved together?

How have you grieved differently?

Love is a fruit of the Holy Spirit at work in a believer's life (Galatians 5:22). If your attitude and love for your husband are not reflecting 1 Corinthians 13, use the space below to repent of any sin, and pray for more love for your spouse.

GOING DEEPER:

Write a note to your spouse to say one thing you appreciate about them. Have an intentional conversation with your spouse about your marriage. Be quick to listen, slow to speak, and slow to get angry (James 1:19).

CAROLINE'S STORY

From the very first day that Andy and I became aware of our Caroline's life, we trusted that God gave her to us for great purpose. We lovingly referred to Caroline as our "bonus baby," since we already had a girl and a boy. Our family was eagerly anticipating her arrival. Our lives changed forever on July 8, 2011, when I went in for a routine appointment and learned of Caroline's fatal diagnosis.

For the most part, my pregnancy had been very similar to my previous two, with the exception of a little relief from the nausea and vomiting. I was still sick, sick, sick, but not to the extent I had been before. It made me a little nervous, but I tried to simply thank God and count it a blessing since I was busy caring for a preschooler and a young toddler.

Within minutes after my appointment began, her sonogram was very concerning—I had no amniotic fluid. My doctor quickly made a few phone calls and arranged for me to see a specialist that afternoon. I tried to remain calm, hoping I was simply a little dehydrated. I chugged a bottle of water as I crossed the street to the specialist's office. I telephoned Andy and tried to fight back fear and hold it together. As I sat waiting in the specialist's office, I began to cry. Though I had feared a miscarriage at times, now that I was more than sixteen weeks pregnant, the fear had dissipated. I had never in my wildest dreams imagined something could be terminally wrong with our unborn baby.

We were told that afternoon that Caroline had a condition called bilateral renal agenesis. Her condition was termed "lethal after birth/incompatible with life outside the womb." Together, Andy and I made a choice that afternoon; we would celebrate our Caroline's little life, no matter how long or short it may be. We fervently began praying for a miracle, but most importantly, we prayed for God's glory to be displayed brightly. We loved her so and were proud to be her parents. Even in the darkness and devastation of that moment, our love for her and for Jesus grew stronger.

We rejoiced as my belly expanded and counted it as great joy when her heartbeat grew stronger each week. We jumped with excitement when we could feel her kick. Doctors predicted very little fetal movement, but she gave us some great kicks that we would cherish forever. We valued time spent talking and singing to her in my belly. We took lots of pictures together, and I journaled a lot. We told our living children about heaven and spent countless hours daydreaming about what heaven was like. Heaven truly is a wonderful place, and we all began to focus on how much we wanted to go there one day.

We chose a special name for our unborn daughter. I had dreamed of having a little girl named Caroline most of my childhood. *Caroline* means "filled with praise." We found great comfort in knowing that she would daily be singing praises to our heavenly Father. We settled on Joy for her middle name, since in the midst of our troubles, we looked to the hope of Christ and the joy that He provided to sustain us. Carrying Caroline challenged our faith, deepened our love for Christ and His people, and created a deep longing within us for heaven.

The Sunday before Caroline's birthday, we stood in front of our church body and shared her story and dedicated her to the Lord for her whole life. We talked about our decision to carry her while she was alive within me, what we had learned through this journey, and how God had demonstrated and filled us with His perfect peace. Andy also shared about how Caroline's life was God's plan A, but our plan B. God was not surprised by her condition. He is the same yesterday, today, and tomorrow. Caroline was our arrow that we were releasing to the Lord, aiming for the bull's-eye and praying for maximal impact.

On October 25, 2011, I gave birth to a beautiful and perfect little girl. She had precious red hair like her daddy and the most angelic face. When she first arrived, she cried the sweetest little cry, and I could imagine her saying, "Ma Ma," in that sweet little voice. It was amazing to see how pink and bright her face was as life was in her.

We had the honor to hold her, pray over her, sing to her, and love her. For those precious moments when it was just her, Andy, and me, we were held intimately together by the love that God had placed within our hearts for one another.

She spent sixty-six minutes with us and then peacefully and quietly went to be with our Lord Jesus. Bedtime is a special time in our home, and that day we took great pleasure in singing her to sleep as she fell asleep in Jesus' arms. We were heartbroken that she had to leave us but filled with the peace that surpasses all understanding because our great God was in control. Knowing she is in heaven with Jesus brings us boundless hope. She knows no pain, knows no sorrow, and dances daily at the feet of her King. Heaven, for our family, became so much sweeter that day. When we pass from this life to the next, she will there waiting for us. October 25 was one of the hardest days of my life, but also one of the most beautiful days of my life. Caroline changed our lives and continues to shape and define us. We count it a true privilege to be Caroline's parents and thank God that He entrusted us with her magnificent little life.

God gave Andy a beautiful mental picture shortly after Caroline's birth. As she passed from this life to the next, he walked her down the aisle to the throne room of God. Standing at the altar was the Lord Jesus, the perfect bridegroom, waiting for his bride. He was ready to take her hand. Just as we hope that one day Andy will hand our living daughters over in marriage to a man here on earth and speak blessings into their lives, Andy took a few moments to speak a blessing into Caroline's life. Then her earthly daddy gave her hand over to her heavenly Daddy. Caroline has always been His from the beginning, and we are deeply grateful for the 236 days and sixty-six minutes God gave her to us.

I had a friend recently compare grief to ocean waves: sometimes it comes and touches your feet gently, and other times it knocks you down so hard. Grief can be messy, lonely, unpredictable, *hard*, and refining. Allow yourself to grieve and to heal. The first year of grief is by far the hardest. I think what has helped Andy and me survive this grief journey is our deep love for Jesus. We know that Jesus created Caroline for a purpose and made no mistakes. She was not an accident or a result of something we did wrong. She was His plan from the very beginning. When things seemed out of control or vulnerable, we quickly directed each other to God's Word. We have disappointed one another along this journey, but our God has never disappointed us. When Jesus is our focus and our hope is found in Him alone, we are able to support one another well as husband and wife. We sought Jesus for our healing, not one another or the things of this world.

We also needed the help of fellow believers. When we were too weak, tired, or sad to pray, they came alongside us and prayed for us, lifting us up to the throne of God. We made a choice to run from self-pity. We made a choice to count Caroline as a gift, not a curse. We are blessed that God allowed us to be Caroline's mom and dad. We deeply desired for our Caroline's little life to have vast impact and meaning. We found grand joy in working together to do something that would honor Caroline and tell others about our Jesus. We chose to build clean water wells in Uganda in Caroline's memory. Our hope is that through our daughter's life and legacy that people in Uganda will drink clean water and hear the truth about the Living Water, Jesus.

Ultimately, we find joy knowing that God used Caroline to develop proven character in us both. He continues to use Caroline's testimony to change others' lives and to transform us spiritually to be more Christlike. We made a choice to allow God to use our baby to change the world, beginning in our own lives. We love to tell others about God's victory in our lives, marriage, and family through a little girl named Caroline. She has changed more lives in her short life than many ever will.

Rejoice in the Lord always. I will say it again: Rejoice!
Let your gentleness be evident to all. The Lord is
near. Do not be anxious about anything, but in every

situation, by prayer and petition, with thanksgiving, present your requests to God. And the peace of God, which transcends all understanding will guard your hearts and your minds in Christ Jesus.
—Philippians 4:4–7 (NIV)

by Lauren Barner, Hope Mom to Caroline

CHAPTER 8

ENGAGING WITH OTHERS

 Do not be overcome by evil, but overcome evil with good.
—Romans 12:21

Have you ever had a bruise that for a brief moment you forgot about, until it was bumped or brushed by something else? Bruises painfully have a way of reminding us of their existence! Grieving hearts are bruised hearts, easily hurt by anything that comes in contact. We have all inevitably been wounded by something that someone has said or done after our baby has fallen asleep.

Whether intentional or not, we have been hurt by others' actions and words or inaction and silence. We have been hurt by things we never even thought could hurt us, and strangers (who *all* seem to be pregnant, of course) have said ridiculous things. It happens because we live around sinners, and sinners sin against each other all the time. Even from those who know you the best, it can be hard to relate, share with, and feel as though they really "get it" and mourn with you.

The past few chapters have been focused on building up your inner woman—establishing a foundation settled on Christ that can handle the waves of grief. In this chapter, we will be studying how we can interact and engage with others around us—our spouse, our children, our parents, our friends—in a right manner.

As we study God's Word, we can depend upon Him for answers to the daily needs of our lives. I pray that this week will open your eyes to how to engage with those around you.

ENGAGING TRUTH

I appeal to you therefore, brothers, by the mercies of God, to present your bodies as a living sacrifice, holy and acceptable to God, which is your spiritual worship. Do not be conformed to this world, but be transformed by the renewal of your mind, that by testing you may discern what is the will of God, what is good and acceptable and perfect.
—Romans 12:1–2

Why are we to present our bodies as a living sacrifice?

How can we be transformed?

What does it mean to "renew your mind," and what is blessing for those that do?

For by the grace given to me I say to everyone among you not to think of himself more highly than he ought to think, but to think with sober judgment, each according to the measure of faith that God has assigned. For as in one body we have many members, and the members do not all have the same function, so we, though many, are one body in Christ, and individually members one of another. Having gifts that differ according to the grace given to us, let us use them: if prophecy, in proportion to our faith; if service, in our serving; the one who teaches, in his teaching; the one who exhorts, in his exhortation; the one who contributes, in generosity; the one who leads, with zeal; the one who does acts of mercy, with cheerfulness.
—Romans 12:3–8

If a Christian, what do these verses say that you have?

What is the big picture of this section of Scripture? (Hint: see verse 5.)

Let love be genuine. Abhor what is evil; hold fast to what is good. Love one another with brotherly affection. Outdo one another in showing honor. Do not be slothful in zeal, be fervent in spirit, serve the Lord. Rejoice in hope, be patient in tribulation, be constant in prayer. Contribute to the needs of the saints and seek to show hospitality.

Bless those who persecute you; bless and do not curse them. Rejoice with those who rejoice, weep with those who weep. Live in harmony with one another. Do not be haughty, but associate with the lowly. Never be conceited. Repay no one evil for evil, but give thought to do what is honorable in the sight of all. If possible, so far as it depends on you, live peaceably with all. Beloved, never avenge yourselves, but leave it to the wrath of God, for it is written, "Vengeance is mine, I will repay, says the Lord." To the contrary, "if your enemy is hungry, feed him; if he is thirsty, give him something to drink; for by so doing you will heap burning coals on his head." Do not be overcome by evil, but overcome evil with good.
—Romans 12:9–21

How many commands can you count in this section? _____

What commands are you obeying? Which are you disobeying?[15]

We obviously want and need others to mourn with us as we grieve our baby. But are we also rejoicing with them, or are we holding them to guilt if they "move on"?

Are you cultivating a heart that waits on the Lord when you feel offended?

The Lord designed us to live in community. He describes His church as a body because in a physical body, every part needs the others. You need others to walk with you during your mourning. Running away from the hurtful situations will not help you grieve. Staying away from pregnant women, or your friend who has a newborn, will only further hurt and alienate you. Allow the Lord to lead you *through* the pain. Hug the pregnant mom. Hold the newborn baby (and cry your eyes out if you need to). But don't run from the pain. Allow God to use the relationships around you to help you heal.

Thank You, Abba, that You love us through other people. Thank You for Your Word, which describes unity and peaceful relationships, and that Your Spirit will enable us to live that way. Would You give us patience when we are offended and courage to reach out, even if we feel like hiding? Please give us peace-filled and encouraging relationships with others. Amen.

REFLECTIONS

Make a list of the encouraging persons in your life. What specific things have they done that have helped you?

Make a list of the challenging or hurtful relationships. What are you doing to obey Romans 12:18, which says to live peaceably with all?

What can you realistically do to reconcile these relationships as much as you are able?

The last verse in Romans 12 states, "Do not be overcome by evil, but overcome evil with good." Fill in the blank for yourself as you reflect on relationships around you. "(Your name), do not be overcome by _____." Are you still struggling with the enemies of the previous chapter? Use the space below to write out a prayer as you reflect on your relationships, asking God to help you relate well to others.

GOING DEEPER:

For the relationships that have been helpful, send them a text, e-mail, or note to say thank you for mourning with you. For the relationships that have been challenging, *pray,* and then pursue peace and reconciliation with them.

NOELLE'S STORY

Bring me guards. Bring me high, sturdy walls. Bring me a moat, and assure me the drawbridge locks. I want safety and protection. Please, do not ask any more of this heart that can hardly feel.

But let me rewind.

My doctors told me that they would allow me to go two weeks "late" while I waited for my daughter to come naturally. On the last possible day prior to my scheduled induction, I went into labor at home—yes, finally! We called the doctor and went to the hospital.

The contractions were mild still, but my husband rolled me into the hospital in a wheelchair. We were familiar with the hospital. Since I was past forty weeks, I had already done three nonstress tests and an extra ultrasound there—in fact, one test was just the night prior. The nurses gave us my favorite, large corner room. I changed into the gown I had bought for labor and then lay on the bed. Everything was familiar: the bands around my belly to keep the monitors, the machines, and the process.

The first nurse could not find a heartbeat. She said that she was new and still learning, but she checked all over—top, bottom, and sides. She left to get another nurse. I looked at my husband, concerned but not yet overly concerned. There was something wrong, like the nurse's technique or the equipment, but certainly not me or my baby. I had just felt my baby move at home and even in the parking lot. My husband gave me a reassuring look.

The second nurse came and quickly checked me with the monitor and left. Something was very wrong, and I could no longer tell myself it was likely the nurse or equipment. I do not remember exactly if my husband and I said anything, but our horror was reflected in each other's faces. A doctor and ultrasound machine materialized more quickly than I knew was possible in a hospital. I had only known hospitals for routine processes and procedures. I had never needed something to happen quickly for me in one. I asked the doctor if there was a heartbeat. He said that he would be able to tell me in a minute.

A minute passed. He paused, and then he looked at us. No, there was no heartbeat for our little girl. Both of the nurses were still in the room. The first, the new trainee nurse, took a few steps back in recognition and I could see her starting to tear up. My husband and I hugged and I cried a screaming cry. My husband cried too, like I had never seen prior to then.

We had waited five years of marriage, for just the right time in our lives, to have our girl. I will never forget the conversation preceding our decision to start trying to conceive. I asked my husband what he wanted to do with his life: dreams, goals, and ambitions. What he said, the only answer he gave, is something I will never forget. He wanted to be a father. It melted my heart.

We could not have been more dedicated to our first child, our girl—our Noelle. The details of labor are vague at best. Three themes that continually circled in my mind were *God is sovereign*, *I need to get my final thoughts in order because I might very well not live through the rest of this* (it seemed fitting that I should not), and *He is carrying me through it because I acted upon strength that I knew was not mine.*

But then she was born. Even though she was not there with us, it was beautiful. I saw her face for the first time—so sweet. The nurses had asked if I wanted to hold her right away after she was born. At first, I said "no". I had already said good-bye, in a way. I had said good-bye to the girl I had only ever known—and only ever wanted to know—as alive. But immediately upon her birth, my thoughts changed because even though she was not really there, part of her was there. I wanted every moment with her I could have. She should have been breathing, crying, and squirming—though her body was perfect, it would never work independently in the world. And still, she was the most beautiful little person I had ever seen.

I knew at this point that I had made it through—that I would probably live. So I knew I would miss her for the rest of my days. My husband held her. He is the positive, upbeat, steady person in our marriage, without a doubt. And knowing his personality, the scene in front of me was not right. That this encouraging, positive, kindhearted person should be holding a daughter who was dead did not compute. But still, I took pictures of him with her as he had already done for me because they were the very best pictures we could have with our best girl. We had done everything so far to the best of our ability with and for her. Surely, we would do no less now in making our final memories.

I was concerned almost from the beginning about giving her body away. I did not know how I could possibly part with her. But the time came. And it came to a moment that felt right because with death's sad decay, she was beginning to look less and less like herself. I knew that my day with her was done. And I thought death could not look worse on a person than on her, a baby whose life should have begun that day. And my heart was overcome with her and for her constantly. Yet I wanted it to fully experience all of the remaining activities that pertained to her. These were what could make it possible: the assurance of His sovereign control over all things at all times, the belief that she went to be with Him, and finally, not necessarily an overwhelming feeling of His presence, but seeing the proof of His presence in the strength I displayed to come through those hours in the hospital.

In the few days following our daughter Noelle's birth into glory, I continued to pray ardently for my heart to be present while I did all of the remaining earthly tasks I could do directly for her. When I came home and recorded the memories of her birth, when I wrote of how much my husband and I missed her, when I finished her pregnancy scrapbook (as though still expecting her) to preserve those now precious thoughts, when I made the announcements for her graveside funeral, when I made a keepsake for family members to take home from the service, when I ordered flowers, when I arranged the program for the service, when I shopped for the outfit in which she would be buried, when I selected the casket and more—in all of it, I prayed for an open, feeling, and available heart. He gave me the strength again: more proof.

And then the funeral was over. The planning was done. I had a list of tasks to do, but they did not elicit in me quite the same inner urgency for presence of heart. Church friends came and so graciously brought us meals. They left them on the front stoop. We retrieved them after their cars pulled away. Mother's Day came just weeks later, and we went out of state to stay in the woods for a while. My heart could no longer be present; I went numb.

So bring me guards. Bring me high, sturdy walls. Bring me a moat and assure me the drawbridge locks. I want safety and protection. Please, do not ask any more of this heart that can hardly feel. This initial alone time was essential—the weeks of private mourning, private prayer, private remembering, and private processing. Those weeks were worth protecting, even though I was really no safer because of them.

Weeks turned to a couple of months, and I needed to fill my time. My heart was open to doing grief God's way, wanting to do it well as unto Him. Even though my heart was numb, I knew my desire to do grief well meant, at least, keeping my heart open. I took inventory of my passions, and without really knowing what I was doing, I started a photography business and made photographing newborns my goal. I needed it. And somehow, some way—actually in a way I do not still experience with the business—I received bookings for newborns from seemingly nowhere (more proof of His presence). I needed to see that though this sinful, broken world damaged the rest of my life with loss, there were others who went without experiencing this damage. Sometimes—thankfully, most of the time—it *does* work the right way. Pregnant mothers go into labor, drive to the hospital or call the midwife to their home, go through labor, and hear a crying, living baby on the other side of it. With tears of joy and love, they feel some of those very first baby breaths on their chest. They take photographs of these fresh moments, knowing that they are the first photographs of many that will be taken over the course of their child's life. They anticipate the future with joy. It's not all broken. The world is so broken, but by the sovereign grace of God, not *all* of it is broken.

The newborn sessions consistently brought rewards into my life. In each one, the parents were warm with joy. They watched us work as my mom (newborn whisperer/assistant) dressed and positioned the babies while I helped and gave instructions to achieve the best photograph I could take. They watched as we put their babies in cute positions and adorned them with darling props, telling us how sweet and adorable they knew these pictures would be. They were thrilled when I, because I felt completely "in it" with them, returned the pictures within a day or so instead of the standard two weeks I promised in business terms. They tagged themselves and their family members when I put the pictures on Facebook. They changed their profile pictures and cover photos to reflect their new, little baby. Friends and family gushed over it all.

This is not all that I did with my time in those days. I also *grieved*. I used my camera to grieve. I remember one picture in particular of my wedding dress next to the white, delicate baby dress I had purchased for Noelle to wear at her dedication service. Would my girl have worn Mamma's wedding dress? I would never know. I cried with people who missed my girl with me. When songs were sung in church about heaven, I would stop singing; not one more word could come. Heaven was all too precious to me to even be spoken of in those days. But during my newborn photography sessions, I did not cry. I did not have to, because their joy actually became my joy. I relished the joy of new life with them and was so grateful to even be able to increase it by some measure.

God did not have to arrange human experience this way. He could have given commandments that He expected us to follow, such as this: "Rejoice with those who rejoice." End of story. But He is gracious. He made His commandments to be life-giving.

I no longer need my own fortress because when He is involved and invited near, safety—humanly speaking—becomes exposed as an illusion. I could not keep my child safe from death. I could not keep my heart safe from insensitivities that inevitably did come my way. Still, I had safety—not mine but His. His will is safe. His will is more powerful than mine. His will provided for me what I did not even know I needed. He is my fortress. My life has become even more proof of it.

So in the end, what becomes of the self-reliant safety I could have prolonged after my trip to the woods? Even more than an illusion, if I had barricaded myself from enough of the world to keep myself free from pain and insensitivities, that same barricade would have done me harm by keeping me from the provisions of God. He gave me joy when I engaged with others who had new babies, which helped to restore my numb heart to life again.

Dismiss the guards. Remove the walls. Drain the moat, and unlock the gate. There is nothing more of me to give. But there is a God, a great fortress, who is gracious enough to give to each heart that is willing to receive and prove that there is no safer place than in Him.

by Lianna Davis, Hope Mom to Noelle

CHAPTER 9

YOUR PLATFORM FOR THE GOSPEL

 Only let your manner of life be worthy
of the gospel of Christ.
—Philippians 1:27a

All of us at one point or another have asked, "Why?" Asking why when you are heartbroken isn't unspiritual. However, if asking this question pushes us farther from God rather than drawing us closer to Him, it is an unhelpful and probably wrong question to be asking.

Too often we tend to accuse God. "Why did this happen? Why didn't You stop this? Why weren't my prayers answered?" In most situations, nothing positive can come from whatever answer there might be to a why question. Even if God gave us His reason why, we would scoff. His reasons, from our limited perspective, would always fall short. Our flat human perceptions cannot process God's multidimensional, eternal reason and perfect will.

Imagine trying to explain gravity to your four-year-old nephew. It's a true concept and one that he will eventually grasp. But right now as he wants to leap from his bunk bed to the floor in a rendition of Superman, he will soar and fall, most likely injuring himself. He wants to know *why* he cannot fly. He's angry and hurt and has a disappointed hope. Even if you patiently explain, he can't grasp the heavier concept of gravity and aerodynamics.

In a much more profound way, God sees us as a precious four-year-old. We cannot grasp the big picture, but beloved, there *is* one. Isaiah 55:8–9 states, "For my thoughts are not your thoughts, neither are your ways my ways, declares the Lord. For as the heavens are higher than the earth, so are my ways higher than your ways and my thoughts than your thoughts." And in Lamentations 3, we are told that God does not willingly grieve the children of men.

Forever asking why will not give you resolution or hope. But if you dare to ask the Lord, "What, Father? What would you have me do with this?" you can rest assured that through His Word, He will give you an answer.

You have a platform to a watching world. If you have identified yourself as a Christian, others are already observing your life and making assumptions about what it means to be a believer in Jesus and how to respond to life circumstances, especially now. One of the questions from the first week of our study was "How do I want this loss to shape the woman I become?" Do you remember what you wrote?

This chapter is about considering "What do I want the world to know about God because of me?" Our lives are already proclaiming our theology, whether or not we believe in the good, enduring character of God; whether or not we believe and set our hope on a life and eternity yet to come; and whether or not we believe that God's Word is applicable to every circumstance, heartbreak, and joy.

This chapter's benefit will rest largely on your own self-introspection and evaluation. I pray that it will be bright, lightening your eyes to the hope of the gospel and fueling you to use these short days for His glory as you draw closer and closer to eternity.

ENGAGING TRUTH

Blessed be the God and Father of our Lord Jesus Christ, the Father of mercies and God of all comfort, who comforts us in all our affliction, so that we may be able to comfort those who are in any affliction, with the comfort with which we ourselves are comforted by God. For as we share abundantly in Christ's sufferings, so through Christ we share abundantly in comfort too.
—2 Corinthians 1:3–5

What do we learn about God from this passage?

What does God do for believers?

Comfort is not meant to be hoarded. What are we to do instead?

For to me to live is Christ, and to die is gain. If I am to live in the flesh, that means fruitful labor for me. Yet which I shall choose I cannot tell. I am hard pressed between the two. My desire is to depart and be with Christ, for that is far better. But to remain in the flesh is more necessary on your account. Convinced of this, I know that I will remain and continue with you all, for your progress and joy in the faith, so that in me you may have ample cause to glory in Christ Jesus, because of my coming to you again.

Only let your manner of life be worthy of the gospel of Christ, so that whether I come and see you or am absent, I may hear of you that you are standing firm in one spirit, with one mind striving side by side for the faith of the gospel, and not frightened in anything by your opponents. This is a clear sign to them of their destruction, but of your salvation, and that from God. For it has been granted to you that for the sake of Christ you should not only believe in him but also suffer for his sake, engaged in the same conflict that you saw I had and now hear that I still have.
—Philippians 1:21–30

Paul longs to be with Christ, but he knows he will stay here on earth a while. What is his reaction to the delay of his hopes?

What is the mandate for the church? (Hint: see verse 27.)

How can we live worthy of the gospel?

What does it mean to suffer for the sake of Christ?

Look again at 2 Corinthians 1:5. What do we receive when we suffer as Christians?

Your platform doesn't need to be big in order to be profound. You don't need to start an international relief organization or become a best-selling author in order for your baby's life and your grief to matter. They already do. As we studied in Psalm 139, your life and your baby's life have inherent value because they were created by the Lord. Your story is already impacting those around you. All you have to do is open your heart and your mouth and share how God is leading you through this valley and what He is teaching you along the way.

Abba, thank You for comforting us with the comfort of Christ and enabling us to give that rest to others. Would You equip this dear sister to live her story well, tenderly trusting You on this journey, as every step brings her closer to seeing her little one again? We praise You for being faithful, and for giving us hope. Amen.

REFLECTIONS

Would you say that you are asking the "Why?" or the "What now?" question?

Are you accepting or despising your platform of loss?

What has your grief said about your theology to those around you?

When you consider how you can comfort others or allow God to use your story to His glory, does anything specific come to mind?

GOING DEEPER:

Allowing the Lord to use your story as a platform for the gospel happens as you make simple, day-to-day choices to trust Him—on the hard days and the good ones. Write, draw, or create art with the phrase "I choose hope" and place it somewhere that you'll be reminded every day that He will care for you.

CHASE'S STORY

In February 2009, my husband and I discovered that we were expecting our fourth baby. We had been in prayer about where the Lord was leading us as a family of five and weren't sure what was in our future at that time. When we found out this baby was on the way, we were surprised … and nervous … and excited.

A few months later, in July, we found out this little one was a *boy*, after having three precious daughters. It seemed that the whole world rejoiced! I, however, was not sure about this turn of events. I immediately became overwhelmed with the idea of raising a son! This was not because I didn't want a boy; I just wanted so badly to do it right. It felt so significant, and it was such a heavy responsibility. We began praying *that* day that we would raise a son to make a difference in his world, to be a leader for the Lord, and to love God with all his heart.

God certainly answered those prayers, and Chase Allen Jacobs *has* made a huge impact on the world—but not at all in the way we had planned.

On September 27, 2009, just four weeks away from what would have been the day of his birth, we got the news that any parent dreads. After a few hours of not feeling our son move, we went to Labor & Delivery on Sunday night and found out that our sweet son had passed from this earth. We found out later that Chase had a blood clot in his umbilical cord and that he most likely put continued pressure on his own cord in some way, blocking the blood supply he needed for life.

At the suggestion of our dear doctor, who had also delivered our three girls over the years, we waited three days to deliver our sweet boy. After that time of preparation, we spent the day surrounded by family who loved us well. We spent hours holding our Chase Allen and taking in all that we could about who he was. It wasn't enough time. Every minute reminded us that he was no longer here and that was an unbearable reality to face.

His life was too short from our perspective. But from God's perspective, Chase's life was not over. He was fully alive and in the arms of His Father, and although I couldn't see it then, the Lord has shown me that truth repeatedly in the months and years since then. The same God who formed and made this precious boy was also fulfilling a plan of redemption He had for that same little boy—and for all of us—even if the story looked much different from how I expected or planned.

Even today, years later, we carry the weight of loss—of life "not as it should be"—and at the very same time, we carry a story of grace, beauty, and healing that He has provided. We still long for our son. Yet in the midst of a grief so deep, God has proven that He is truly the God of all comfort and that He always redeems what is broken in our lives. We can trust Him to not only meet us in our pain but also to change us to look more like His Son through it.

Weeks after we said good-bye (for now) to our son, my husband prayed a prayer that we have repeated again and again since then.

> Lord, we long to be wholly and completely Yours, in pain and in joy. We never want to go back to the people we used to be, because we want Chase to have changed us. We feel closer to Your heart now, even as we walk this valley. Lord, we beg You to never let us return to normal again.

I want to share with you how He has changed us through that prayer, through grief, and through His comfort.

Before God changed me, I always walked in fear. I was a self-defined worrywart. I was the person who hovered over my children, who always imagined the worst-case scenario and played the what-if game about what tragedy might enter my life at some point. I have always worried about the day when something bad would happen.

I remember hearing about the losses of others—and even how they were strengthened through them—and it only made me think, *I could never get through that! I'm not strong enough!"* I remember hearing, "Someday you will walk through a valley. Some loss, some struggle, some tragedy *will* happen to you." I'm sure you've heard it too. It's not a matter of *if;* it's *when.*

I had also heard this thought many times before: *When trials come, you have to be prepared spiritually in advance. You have to be armed for the hard times before they come.* I had always asked myself, "Am I ready? Am I spiritually armed for my time of suffering? Sure, I know Scripture, I know who God is, and I have a relationship with Him, but am I ready? I'm still so afraid! How do I know if I'm strong enough?"

This is where my theology was wrong. The truth that God has allowed me to realize over these years of walking with Him through grief is that we will *never* be strong enough on our own. He never asked us to be. You may not have been ready for what awaited you in this life, but God was.

He was not surprised when my Chase passed from this life into His arms. In fact, He had begun preparing the way for me long before. He was orchestrating the events of those days, so that I would see—without any doubt—that *His* strength is truly made perfect in my weakness. He longed to comfort me in ways that proved that *His* hands were holding me up and that *His* peace was filling my soul in ways that brought Him glory.

No, I was not strong enough. I was not ready. But God was. I look back on what has been the hardest valley of my life, and although there was deep sadness and pain, there has also been such peace because He was there in every moment, every decision, and every conversation.

He provided for us in the valley, and He hasn't stopped.

I didn't really know that truth until I lost a child. I don't know that I believed fully and totally that God is our strength. His power is made perfect in our weakness. And He is our only steadfast hope.

In a way, He has proven Himself to me in the darkness, so that I can walk with Him more securely in the light. Before, I lived in fear. Today, I live in confidence. I long to share the greatness and glory of who He is more than I ever did before. I want my life to reflect the power of what He has done for me, when I was too weak to do any of it on my own.

Our "family verse of hope" that we have clung to since the night after we said good-bye to our Chase is from Psalm 33.

> We wait in hope for the LORD; he is our help and
> our shield. In him our hearts rejoice, for we trust
> in his holy name. May your unfailing love be with
> us, LORD, even as we put our hope in you.
> —Psalm 33:20–22 (NIV)

As He was teaching me these truths about His heart and helping us through the sorrow in our own, He was also beginning to weave a story we could never have imagined.

As parents who had just lost a child, we felt helpless and completely out of control. Our plans had changed. Our world had been rocked. And the only thing left to do was ask for His direction from here. All we could do was give it all to Him and say, "We trust You. Help us. Use us. Make this glorify You." So our prayers became about His glory and not just about us. He began showing us His plan for us, and as we continued to be open to His guidance, He began showing us quite obviously and plainly what His desire was for our family.

It was to take care of His other children.

Through a series of events, we felt God calling us to take care of His children who are still here, and who still need Him in their lives. We know where our Chase is, and the Lord was comforting us even while we felt the giant void in our lives. In that brokenness, He showed us other children who are in desperate need of Christ too.

He had more planned for Chase's life and for our family, and He was giving us a platform to share His gospel through our brokenness, through our loss, and through our lives.

He knew that what lay ahead of us was even greater than our suffering. And as Corrie ten Boom says in her book *The Hiding Place*, "Every experience God gives us, every person He puts in our lives is the perfect preparation for a future that only He can see."[16]

We were being prepared for something. We could feel it. As Ephesians 2:10 (NIV) says, "For we are God's handiwork, created in Christ Jesus to do good works, which God prepared in advance for us to do."

So He continued to speak through His Word and reveal His plan. Then He gave us an answer to dealing with our grief. Isaiah 58 says,

> Loose the chains of injustice ... set the oppressed free ... share your food with the hungry ... provide the poor wanderer with shelter ... *Then your light will break forth like the dawn,* and your healing will quickly appear; then your righteousness will go before you, and the glory of the Lord will be your rear guard. Then you will call, and the Lord will answer; you will cry for help, and he will say: Here am I ... and if you spend yourselves in behalf of the hungry and satisfy the needs of the oppressed, then your light will rise in the darkness, and your night will become like the noonday. The Lord will guide you always; he will satisfy your needs in a sun-scorched land and will strengthen your frame.
> —Isaiah 58:6,7,8-11 (NIV, emphasis mine)

The way He knew our night would become like noonday was through taking care of His other children across the world, the ones who were hungry, oppressed, and hopeless.

Our child died even with access to the best health care in the world. I had the best doctor caring for me and the highest quality medicines available to me. Yet Chase still passed away. But God was showing us something significant: there are children all over this world who have survived the worst of conditions, who were made in God's image just as Chase was, and who have a purpose which God created them for.

Our hearts were breaking, and God was doing it. He was lifting the veil that had covered our eyes, and we could now see the need. We could see how Chase's life could be honored by helping other children thrive, and we could see how His glory could be *great* as we comfort others with His comfort (2 Corinthians 1:4).

Since those early days of revelation, we have been blessed to follow His call to start a ministry for orphaned and abandoned children in Rwanda. From those earliest moments, when friends joined us in sponsoring children's medical care and school costs as a way to honor Chase, God has grown those tiny efforts into a nonprofit foundation that provides for the needs of 250 children from an overcrowded orphanage. They otherwise had no hope.

Since God started us on this journey, we have traveled a dozen times to Africa, a place I never imagined I would go! Now I constantly long for the moment when we will return again.

Since the day I held my own son's hand for the last time, I have held the hands of countless child slaves. Since the day I kissed my own son's face after he died, I have kissed the faces of hundreds of abandoned babies and children. Since the day I stood in my own dark valley, I have stood in the middle of orphanages loving on dirty, needy kids. I've been made completely "uncomfortable" by American standards. I have been absolutely emptied out. And I have never felt such joy, such absolute assurance, that I was right where I was supposed to be.

Through the loss of a child, I have grieved—and been comforted—in ways I never thought possible. But I've also received the Lord's fullness of joy in ways I never could have before. And as He strengthened me and walked with me, I fell in love with Him for the first time in my life. I found myself surrendering my way for His—and I found blessings of new life and new vision! Oh, how the Lord longs to fill us up, when we are emptied out before Him! And oh, the miracles we experience when we let Him lead!

> You have made known to me the path of *[my]*
> life; you will fill me with joy in Your presence,
> with eternal pleasures at your right hand.
> —Psalm 16:11 (NIV, emphasis mine)

As mothers enduring the loss of our children, we grieve and we suffer. As a result, we have an opportunity that many do not: we know what it feels to be broken, and we can now genuinely love others who are broken and lost. We can choose to join Him in sharing the gospel of His hope with those who also need His healing. This is a privilege that He has entrusted to us, although it involves pain we never wished for.

None of us know what the end of our story will look like. Even now, as we run a ministry for orphans and do our best to share the good news of God's love with others, my husband and I don't know what obstacles we will face-- or what valleys we may yet find ourselves in. But we know who leads every step of the way, and we know that He is the one and only source of comfort and strength we need.

Because of that truth, and the comfort He has given, our family will continue saying yes to His purposes for our lives, no matter the road that takes us there. And we thank Him that, through a broken heart, we could join Him in caring for what breaks His heart.

by Chelsea Jacobs, Hope Mom to Chase

JOURNEYING ON

As Gwendolyn's first birthday drew near, I was a constant mess of emotions. The first year of all the "little deaths"—the moments when I had to be reminded again and again that she wasn't here—had been exhausting and heartbreaking, yet healing. I had grown more in my understanding of God in one year than the twenty-seven years before it. My husband and I had grieved hard, but grieved with hope. I had often asked the Lord to reveal Himself to me tangibly, to speak a word of comfort, to show Himself to me. The night before her first birthday, I had a glorious realization. God had loved me through one thousand faces. Through every person who had prayed for me, brought us meals, cried with us, given us flowers, sent books and gifts, remembered the hard days, cleaned our house, and served us in big and small ways, God was moving through them. Psalm 77:19 talks about God leading His people Israel through the deep, "yet your footprints were unseen." God's work in us is often unseen, but it is happening all the same.

Psalm 147:3 states, "He heals the brokenhearted and binds up their wounds." I pray that through this study you have drawn nearer to Him through reading His Word, allowing Him to wash and cleanse your battered heart as He gently binds you up and heals you.

As you lift up your eyes to the days ahead, take courage. God has not left you alone. When you're facing your first round of holidays without your little one, He will carry you through. When you are making decisions about growing your family again, He will give guidance. If you are faced with the reality that another biological child might not be what He has for you, He will sustain. As each day draws to an end, take comfort. You are one day closer to heaven, to your little one, and to being in complete joy in the presence of Christ.

You keep him in perfect peace
whose mind is stayed on you,
because he trusts in you.
Trust in the Lord forever,
for the Lord God is an everlasting rock.
—Isaiah 26:3–4

REFLECTIONS

Look back over your study notes and journal questions from the last few chapters. What part of this study impacted you?

As you look toward the days ahead, what causes the most anxiety? What gives you joy?

Reflect on your answers from the very first questions: "How do you want this loss to shape the woman you become? In ten years, what words do you want to describe you?" Is your answer to that the same, or has it changed? How are you growing more toward becoming a Christlike woman?

LEADER'S GUIDE

The goal for this study is to help grieving moms grow in their understanding of biblical truth in light of their grief and give them a close-knit community to encourage them along the way. We cannot grieve well until we know the truth. And the only truth that exists is what God has set forth in His Word, the Bible. That will be our foundation. Not modern psychology or stages of grief, even if those can sometimes aid the understanding of man's natural response to tragedy. The foundation that will last is built on God's character and His Word (Matthew 7:24–27).

The following is a suggested sequence for a small group time:

ICEBREAKERS

Give the women an opportunity to get to know one another and each other's stories. On your first time together, take time to share about your Hope Babies and how they're currently doing. For future gatherings, have the moms bring any photos or mementos they want to share, or open with non-grief-related questions (e.g., "Where did you last vacation?" and "What was the highlight of your week?").

PRAYER

Open your time with prayer, led either by you or another woman in your group, and be sure to end your time together with prayer as well.

Bring index cards and have the women write their prayer requests on them before you begin; then have everyone pick one up before leaving and pray for that specific woman and her need during the week.

DISCUSSION

Be personal with your discussion, but also keep on topic. Make sure everyone has time to share. You will need to keep the flow moving so that you can get into the "Engaging Truth" and "Going Deeper" content.

ENGAGING TRUTH

Have the women bring a Bible, and read some or all of the verses from that week out loud. Ask specific women to respond to the text.

It's easy for us to ask, "How do you *feel* about this verse?" But our feelings are not authoritative. God's Word *is!* Instead, ask questions such as these:

What does this verse(s) teach us about God's character? Or the way that He interacts with mankind?

Our feelings often do not align with what the Bible is saying. Since God's Word is the truth, what are we to do when our feelings say something different?

When you hear unbiblical thinking, respond with biblical truth. You are not a passive facilitator. Don't be afraid to respond to hurt and anger; always bring it back to the Lord. *It's okay to say that you don't know the answer.* But try to find out the answer before y'all meet again.

GOING DEEPER

Always leave them with some point of application from your study. We want to be more than just "hearers of the word, but doers" (James 1:22). Each chapter has a "Going Deeper" section. Feel free to use that or the suggestions in the "Leader's Guide," or creatively tailor it specifically for your group as you get to know them.

KEY VERSE

Each week we will have a key verse, indicated by the anchor, related to the study. Be creative with how you use this! Share it through a social media picture; send it in a postcard; encourage the women to write it out or memorize it; etc. They need to know God's Word and treasure it in their hearts. The Bible is the primary way the Lord speaks to us and how He will bring hope and healing to their lives.

Praise God that His Word never returns void. No matter the outcome of each group, we know that our God hears us and that His Word will produce results. We're praying for your study to be a beautiful and hope-filled time together! Please let us know how we can assist you as you lead.

Because He lives, we hope.
Hope Mommies leadership team

The goal for your first session is to break the ice and get to know each other. How you start out this week will determine the course of your group. Let the women share their stories. Bring Kleenex and cookies, and as you share, keep a list of each Hope Mom and the name(s) of her babies. Make sure to send a copy to each woman in your group so she can be praying for each mom and her story by name.

GOING DEEPER

If they've read the "Introduction," have them write a letter to themselves with the five words that they want to describe their future self in ten years. At the bottom of the letter, have the women write, "Am I closer to becoming this?" and seal the letters. At the end of your study together, hand them back their letters.

The underlying idea of this question is to help the women see that the natural bent of a broken, sinful heart is probably *not* what they want for their lives. Do they want to stay married? Do they want to have joy? Do they want their living children to feel loved and precious? Do they still want to keep their friends—the ones who haven't experienced infant loss? Those things take work; they will not come with time. They are the fruit of a heart that chooses to trust God and brokenly approach Him, allowing Him to heal them in His timing.

CHAPTER 1

MARKED BY LOSS

Your eyes saw my unformed substance;
in your book were written, every one of them,
the days that were formed for me,
when as yet there were none of them.
—Psalm 139:16

DISCUSSION

How have they felt marked by loss?

ENGAGING TRUTH

Read Psalm 139 together and have volunteers share their answers to the study questions.

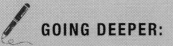

GOING DEEPER:

Give each woman a piece of paper and a marker. Have her write, "I feel marked by _____," and fill in the blank. On the other side of the paper, have her write, "But today I choose to believe _____." If they're stumped on what to write, fill in with what you learned from the lesson: God is loving, God has a plan, God knows everything, etc.

CHAPTER 2

WHAT ABOUT GOD?

My soul melts away for sorrow; strengthen
me according to your word!
—Psalm 119:28

DISCUSSION

Recap last week. Was there anything that was specifically encouraging to you?

How would you describe your relationship with God before your loss?

What characteristics would you have attributed to God before your loss? Have those changed at all?

ENGAGING TRUTH

Read Psalm 119:68, Jeremiah 32:17, and 2 Timothy 3:16–17 together, and have volunteers share their answers to the study questions.

GOING DEEPER:

Choose one aspect of God's character to focus on this week. Share it with your spouse, with friends and family, on your social media, etc. Look up other verses that support that doctrine. Put it out there as a reminder to believe, even on days when believing is hard.

CHAPTER 3

WRESTLING WITH DISAPPOINTMENT, DOUBT, AND FEAR

Even though I walk through the valley
of the shadow of death,
I will fear no evil, for you are with me;
your rod and your staff, they comfort me.
—Psalm 23:4

DISCUSSION

Recap last week. What part of God's character did you choose to think on this past week? What did you learn or discover from this past week?

Can you relate to the disappointment, doubt, and fear discussed in this chapter?

ENGAGING TRUTH

Read Lamentations 3:17–33 out loud and discuss the study questions.

GOING DEEPER:

Choose a verse from this week's study to *write on your heart*. Commit it to memory, and repeat it aloud when you feel doubt and fear begin to creep in. Share it with your group.

CHAPTER 4

HEAVEN AND ETERNITY

 But our citizenship is in Heaven, and from it we await a Savior, the Lord Jesus Christ, who will transform our lowly body to be like his glorious body, by the power that enables him even to subject all things to himself.
—Philippians 3:20–21

DISCUSSION

How does our culture (media, merchandise, worldviews, etc.) portray eternity and heaven?

What does our culture believe about who gets to go to heaven?

What is your earliest memory or thought about death and heaven?

What ridiculous thing has someone told you about death or heaven? What has someone told you that was encouraging?

ENGAGING TRUTH

Read aloud some of the verses that you studied that week. Discuss their understanding of heaven and eternity. Questions to ask may be these:

What did you learn about heaven that you didn't know before?

Do you believe that you will go to heaven? Why or why not?

GOING DEEPER:

Go to the place where you are reminded the most of your baby (cemetery, garden, nursery room, hospital, etc.) and read 1 Corinthians 15 out loud. Praise God for His truth, tell Him what is difficult, and pour out your heart to Him.

CHAPTER 5

BIBLICAL MOURNING IS
ROOTED IN HOPE

 But we do not want you to be uninformed, brothers, about those who are asleep, that you may not grieve as others do who have no hope.
—1 Thessalonians 4:13

DISCUSSION

Recap. Did they get to go to the cemetery/memorial and read 1 Corinthians 15? How was that experience?

What has been one helpful outlet for your grief (journaling, church, reading, counseling, etc.)?

Define the word *hope* in your own words.

ENGAGING TRUTH

Have volunteers read, or ask specific women to read aloud 1 John 1:9, Psalm 145:14, 1 Thessalonians 4:13–18, Psalm 5:1–3, Psalm 18:1–6, and Psalm 130 and discuss how they demonstrate hope in God.

GOING DEEPER:

Write a note of encouragement to another woman in the group.

Do a word search online for biblical references on hope. Choose one, write it on a Post-It, and keep it somewhere visible.

CHAPTER 6

ENEMIES OF YOUR SOUL

 You prepare a table before me in the
presence of my enemies.
—Psalm 23:5

In this chapter, we are going to survey Proverbs as it talks about enemies of our souls. A proverb is a statement that is usually of cause and effect. Proverbs are observations of how God deals with His people and how man's sin and righteousness affect individuals. They are not promises per se but are wonderful, factual statements about the Lord and humanity. We will also look at Colossians, at a summary of "enemies," and how the Christian is to respond instead.

My challenge for you leaders is to uncover the opposite of each of these enemies with your group. For example, what is the righteous counterpart to envy? Answer: contentment. Have the women search the Bible to find a biblical response to these specific enemies.

DISCUSSION

In your own words, define envy, anger, bitterness, resentment, and self-pity.

Which of those emotions threaten to overwhelm you, perhaps more than others, as you grieve?

Are there other emotions you're experiencing that you can identify as enemies to your faith?

ENGAGING TRUTH

Identify the enemies in the following verses: Proverbs 14:30, 29:11, and 30:33.

Read Colossians 3:5–15, and answer the study questions.

A FEW NOTES

Pride is often revealed through self-pity. It is an emotion that says, "I deserve better. I shouldn't have to deal with this. I am better than this. I deserve something different." Self-pity thinks more highly of ourselves than we should; self-pity is prideful.

The Bible teaches that sin comes in plurality (James 3:16), and these emotions often flow together; hurt leads to anger, anger to pride and resentment, etc. But it can be helpful to target specific attitudes and sins that are prominent in our lives.

GOING DEEPER:

Spend time praying with another woman in the group about an enemy (sin area) that you deal with the most.

CHAPTER 7

GRIEVING TOGETHER

Love bears all things, believes all things,
hopes all things, endures all things.
—1 Corinthians 13:7

Before you begin the discussion, read Hebrews 13:4 aloud. Also keep in mind that not all of the participants may be married. Lead a grace-filled discussion about their primary relationship. While we want your group to be vulnerable about their relationships and marriages, we also want to hold marriage in high esteem and honor their spouses. Do not allow discussions to become degrading or trespass on too intimate of details. Encourage these women to be honorable in their speech about their husbands.

DISCUSSION

How has your spouse responded to your loss?

What is your communication like now, even about normal things?

On a scale from 1 to 10, with 1 being "nonexistent" and 10 being "completely unified," how would you rate the oneness of your marriage right now, and why?

ENGAGING TRUTH

Review the verses regarding God's goal for marriage (Genesis 2:23–24, Ephesians 5:22–23, 1 Corinthians 13:4–7), and discuss the study questions.

GOING DEEPER:

Read through 1 Corinthians 13 together as a group. Write out one of the aspects of love, and keep it somewhere as a reminder to demonstrate that to their spouse this week.

CHAPTER 8

ENGAGING WITH OTHERS

 Do not be overcome by evil, but overcome evil with good.
—Romans 12:21

This chapter is focused on how we relate to other important relationships in our lives: our family and friends.

The goal of this chapter is to evaluate our own attitudes and responses. It's not a rag session where we can pull out all grievances and feel validated in building a wall against those who have hurt us. Beware of the enemies of chapter 6! Strive to find the balance of vulnerability and honesty as you discuss this chapter's content.

DISCUSSION

Recap last meeting. Share how you related to your spouse since the last time you met. Was it the same, improved, or less than ideal?

Who in your life "gets it" as you mourn? Who understands and mourns well with you?

What has been your response to an offhand or hurtful comment?

ENGAGING TRUTH

Read Romans 12 aloud and discuss the study questions.

GOING DEEPER:

Bring a box of notecards and spend ten to fifteen minutes writing notes. Do they need to say thank-you for someone who has loved them well? Do they need to reconcile with someone? Do they need to seek forgiveness?

CHAPTER 9

YOUR PLATFORM FOR THE GOSPEL

 Only let your manner of life be worthy
of the gospel of Christ.
—Philippians 1:27a

DISCUSSION

As you look back on the last few weeks of our study, which topic has been the most encouraging? What topic has been the most challenging?

What is your initial reaction to the phrase "Do not despise your platform"?

ENGAGING TRUTH

Read 2 Corinthians 1:3–5 and Philippians 1:21–30 aloud, and share your answers to your study questions.

GOING DEEPER:

Share one way that you want to honor your little one.

WRAPPING UP

Get together again as a celebratory wrap-up time. Ideas might be to go out to dinner, have a balloon release for your babies, or host a box gathering and provide hope boxes to your local hospital. End your time with prayer, thanking God for each of these women and the babies that have changed their lives.

APPENDIX A

ANGELS AND BABIES

It's a misconception to assume that our babies are now angels. Once we understand what the Bible really says about angels, we can rejoice that our babies are still persons and not winged infants playing harps while resting on clouds.

In *Systematic Theology: An Introduction to Biblical Doctrine*, Wayne Grudem summarizes the biblical descriptions of angels. "Angels are created, spiritual beings with moral judgment and high intelligence, but without physical bodies."[17]

The Hope Mommies' Doctrinal Statement says we believe angels are individual beings capable of reasoning, speech, and interaction and are not deceased humans. Angels active on earth are normally invisible to human eyes. They are sent out by God in response to prayer and/or God's commands, and they wage war on behalf of God and men against demons as well as serve the elect in ways consistent with the will of God. Angels can take on physical form and appear as humans. We can respond to or interact with angels, unaware of their identity (Dan. 8:16–26; Luke 1:26–38; Dan. 10:13, 21; 2 Kings 6:17; Dan. 9:21, 23; 10:12–13; Rev. 12:7; Gen. 18–19; Heb. 1:14, 13:2).

ENDNOTES

1. The New Testament speaks of the death of a believer as having fallen asleep and says that true death is separation from God for all eternity. However, if you have put your faith in Jesus Christ and repented of sin, then physical death is not an eternal death. It is as though you have "fallen asleep" and Christ will one day cause you to wake again (Psalm 116:15; 1 Corinthians 15:17–22; 1 Thessalonians 4:13–14). See chapter 4 on heaven and eternity to learn more about the death of believers and of infants.

2. Tozer, A. W. *The Knowledge of the Holy: The Attributes of God, Their Meaning in the Christian Life.* New York: Harper & Row, 1961, 1.

3. Grudem, Wayne A. "Moral Attributes: Goodness." *Systematic Theology: An Introduction to Biblical Doctrine.* Leicester, England: Inter-Varsity, 1994, 197.

4. "Carlsbad Caverns National Park." *Wikipedia.* Wikimedia Foundation. Accessed December 16, 2014.

5. "Resources: Bible Introductions: Lamentations." *Lamentations.* GTY.org. Accessed December 15, 2014.

6. "Americans Describe Their Views about Life after Death." Barna.org. The Barna Group, Ltd., October 21, 2013. Accessed November 25, 2014.

7. Alcorn, Randy. *Heaven.* Carol Stream, Illinois: Tyndale, 2004, 54.

8. For additional reading on the biblical evidence for infants in heaven, see John MacArthur's *Safe in the Arms of God.*

9. Alcorn, Randy. *Heaven: Biblical Answers to Common Questions.* Carol Stream, Illinois: Tyndale, 2004, 9.

10. Maybe mosquitos will exist on the new earth, but they certainly will not cause pain! For a thorough explanation on the renewed earth, please see Randy Alcorn's book titled *Heaven.*

11. "Hope." Dictionary.com. Unabridged. Random House, Inc. Accessed December 5, 2014.

12. Cushman, Erin L. "Blessed Hope: Hope Mommies." Blogspot.com, December 23, 2010. Accessed December 5, 2014.

13. Sexual intimacy following a loss can be an area fraught with emotional landmines. For many women, intimacy isn't physically possible for a few weeks. The goal of sexuality is to reaffirm your oneness, love, and emotional transparency together. If you're unable to be physically intimate, talk with your spouse. Reaffirm your devotion and oneness in other ways.

14. It is not the goal of this Bible study to launch into the lengthy discussion of biblical womanhood and submission, though we encourage you to read *Feminine Appeal* by Carolyn Mahaney and *Recovering Biblical Manhood and Womanhood,* edited by John Piper and Wayne Grudem, to understand the God-given roles for wives. We will state that submission never means staying in an abusive relationship. If you are in a physical or emotionally abusive relationship, please seek the counsel of a Bible-believing church, and get help from local authorities if you or your children are in danger.

15. Obedience is only possible with the indwelling of God's Holy Spirit, who He has generously given to all who have placed their faith in Jesus Christ. If you have not repented of your sin and trusted in Jesus for salvation from that sin, then it will be impossible for you to obey God's Word and exhibit the genuine fruit of His Spirit in your life. If you have questions about your salvation and relationship with God and want to talk with someone, please contact the Hope Mommies leadership team at info@hopemommies.org.

16. Ten Boom, Corrie. *The Hiding Place.* Peabody, Massachusetts: Hendrickson Publishers, 2011, X.

17. Grudem, Wayne A. "Angels: Explanation and Scriptural Basis." *Systematic Theology: An Introduction to Biblical Doctrine.* Leicester, England: Inter-Varsity, 1994, 397.

Printed in the United States
By Bookmasters